T0067188

The Happy Home

YOUR GUIDE TO CREATING A
HAPPY, HEALTHY, WEALTHY LIFE

Patricia Lohan

BALBOA.PRESS

A DIVISION OF HAY HOUSE

Balboa Press books may be ordered through
booksellers or by contacting:

Balboa Press
A Division of Hay House
1663 Liberty Drive
Bloomington, IN 47403
www.balboapress.com.au
AU TFN: 1 800 844 925 (Toll Free inside Australia)
AU Local: (02) 8310 7086 (+61 2 8310 7086 from outside Australia)

Print information available on the last page.

ISBN: 978-1-5043-1558-6 (sc)
ISBN: 978-1-5043-1559-3 (e)

Balboa Press rev. date: 12/02/2022

For women around the world
who are dedicated to creating a happy home
and ultimately a happy, healthy, wealthy life.

CONTENTS

PART 1   THE POWER OF FENG SHUI

PART 2   FENG SHUI FLOW

PART 3 FENG SHUI FOR YOUR HOUSE

PART 4 FENG SHUI ROOM BY ROOM

PART 5   POWERFUL FENG SHUI FOR YOU

PREFACE

What the hell am I doing with my life?

That's what I was thinking as I was cycling around Dublin on a borrowed bicycle back when I was a single healer and yoga teacher. Some days I was earning as little as €5 a day. I was working hard on myself and my business, reading self-help books, saying mantras, writing affirmations, and buying personal development courses. But I was still stuck, worrying about money, and having no luck in the love department. It was hard. My vision for my life was just so much ... *bigger.* I felt like I was playing small just teaching yoga, doing sound healings, and selling knick knacks, while longing to have an amazing business, live somewhere nice, and break away from the 'smaller' version of me. I just couldn't figure out what to do, or how to break through.

Have you been here yourself?

How do you go from there, to attracting a husband and soulmate, turning your passion into a success, and becoming a role model to thousands of women around the globe?

The game-changer for me, *in every part of my life*, was Feng Shui.

I was fifteen when I got my first Feng Shui book – I've always loved it. I grew up with entrepreneurial parents who worked all the time, running their businesses. All I ever knew was business, and I always had a job, right from the age of seven or eight. As far back as I can remember, they ran restaurants, pubs, guesthouses, and hotels. When I was eighteen, we were running a small hotel. I brought a Feng Shui expert to Galway, my hometown, to Feng Shui my parents' new house. I remember believing at the time, "Feng Shui is really good for business", and convincing my parents to hire her!

Then life took me on a very different path where I 'forgot' about my passion for Feng Shui. I moved to Dublin, where it felt like I was starting from scratch. I wondered if I'd ever move abroad again, meet 'the one', or be capable of earning more than €5 in a day.

Despite being immersed in personal development, I couldn't figure out why I couldn't break through and just be successful. Despite my sunny spirit, I was caught in a daily pattern of fear. I was single. I was broke.

It seemed like the perfect time to give Feng Shui another try.

When I first got to Dublin, I couldn't afford to live alone, so I slept in a friend's apartment and borrowed another friend's bicycle to get around. I was grateful for my friend's apartment, for my family, and for my deep desire to make a difference in the world, even though I wasn't sure how I would do that. I knew I wanted to earn more money and find my soulmate, so I trusted the process and my circumstances started to change.

Instead of focusing on what I didn't have, I spent my energy showing gratitude for everything I did have. Incredible things started happening. For one, I manifested my dream apartment by writing a wish list. I started to see how important it was to hold an intention in my mind.

My new home needed to focus on my current vision and there was only one way I knew to make that happen. Feng Shui. I started implementing Feng Shui as soon as I moved in, digging out the books I had been given on my fifteenth birthday, removing negative energy, and creating my remedy for success.

Determined to attract the right person, I Feng Shui-ed my bedroom for love. Soon after, I met Ken, my now-husband, and he told me he had Feng Shui-ed his bedroom for love too. As coincidence upon coincidence came, I finally saw that Feng Shui *was* the answer ... and it was my chance.

After seeing my results, I followed my heart to blend my healing practices with Feng Shui and have since created the exact lifestyle I dreamed about back in Dublin: living in beautiful warm Bali & New York. Summers in Greece, travelling around the world, and running a very successful online business that I love, with my husband and soulmate, Ken and Toby.

Sometimes I have to pinch myself and ask if this is real!

I know there are more people out there who are still going through what I was feeling back in Dublin. If my story sounds anything like yours, you're in the right place. You may have done lots of personal development work, creating a vision board that still isn't a reality, been making money or struggling to do so, or having relationships that are tense, frustrating, or non-existent. Well, I am overjoyed to be able to share Feng Shui with you.

You are about to embark on a journey to enhance your home so that it supports you in creating happiness, health, and wealth in your life.

You can have all the blessings, the joy, and the abundance you desire.

It all starts at home.

Love, Patricia xxx

INTRODUCTION

Are things just not going the way you've envisioned? Does it feel like everywhere you turn, no matter what you're doing, there's just no flow?

This may be in different parts of your life. For example, some parts of your life might be flowing well. You might have a wonderful relationship, but your career and sense of purpose might not feel satisfying. Or vice versa, you might be thriving in your career but can't seem to find any luck in love.

Do you feel stuck in certain parts of your life, and they just never seem to budge?

You might be having sleepless nights, worrying about things like children not getting along, your business not growing and evolving as it should, money worries, relationship issues — the list goes on and on.

All of this complies with a complete sense of overwhelm and feeling stressed out.

You might be asking yourself at times, "Is this really it? Is this the life I'm supposed to be living? Is this how it's meant to be?"

If you find yourself waking up, and worrying about all the things that have gone wrong, it might feel nearly impossible to be excited about the future and opportunities in your life. Instead of being excited about your life, it might feel like a never-ending cycle of issues and blocks.

People in your house bickering. Issues in relationships. Never enough money to do the things you really want to do. Or maybe there is enough money, but it comes at the expense of working all day every day and feeling completely burned out.

If this sounds familiar, you might feel that you are stuck, unhappy, and just want more freedom, more love, and more joy. You might see other people thriving in their lives and wonder, "Why not me?"

This chronic lack of flow is costing you your health, your mindset, your time, and your life!

It's a time-sink, where you're spending your days on this wheel of overwhelm and disappointment wondering, "Is this really all there is?"

But here's the truth. You've been brought to this planet with a beautiful opportunity to live an amazing life. Why have you not felt the ability to embrace it? To feel it, to enjoy it, to absolutely savour your experiences?

To savour being a mum. To savour having a business. To love your work, love being around the right people, and have the time and energy to spend with your family. To be able to go on holidays, and not just work, work, work for no real sense of reward.

Let me tell you a story from one of our clients who took her world from zero to hero in less than a year in our PowerHouse Feng Shui programme.

Before she joined, she felt like her life was just a constant stream of stress. Working seventy hours a week (but only getting paid the equivalent of forty), was putting a *huge* strain on her family, the time with her kids and husband, and her own well-being.

As soon as she joined our signature programme, she began to take action, and implement her Feng Shui remedies.

Just after implementing her Feng Shui, she received a massive reduction on her home's mortgage. With a boost in confidence from adding her Feng Shui remedies, she asked her company of fourteen years for a reduction of hours. Thinking they would laugh at her, they surprisingly accepted her proposal! Now she only works twelve hours a week and can drive her kids to school in the morning, have time to do activities for herself, make healthy meals every day, and also have alone time with her husband.

Without the stress in her life, she has been able to plan for wonderful holidays both with her husband and with the whole family, and still has time for her own self-care.

Now, she is the mum and partner she's always wanted to be. Working fewer hours, and still able to go on great holidays, she feels a sense of security and ease in her life.

And what's even more incredible, is that as she implemented the Feng Shui remedies on her own, her husband started to thrive in his job! Yes, that's right. Just from living in a Feng Shui-ed home, her husband's work began to take off.

This is the power of Feng Shui. And this is the magic I'm here to show you.

I am here to tell you that, just like our wonderful PowerHouse member who turned her life into her dream life, you *can* feel a sense of complete security, support, and safety in everything you do. You *can* thrive and actually live your vision board.

I've seen it happen with hundreds of our members on a day-to-day basis.

You don't have to keep feeling that "someday" it will actually be like that. This is it *now*. You can live this *now*. You can experience it *now*.

Maybe you've tried Feng Shui before and it hasn't worked. Or, maybe you've implemented a few things and you haven't noticed any results. Perhaps your friends and family may be sceptical about Feng Shui, or people you live with might feel reluctant to change anything in your home. You, yourself, might even be afraid that you'll have to make big, structural changes to your home.

Working with Feng Shui is really just about creating energetic support for your home.

Your home *can* be happy, joyful, and a great place to be. It is possible for you to love being at home. To love spending time with your family, and for your home to be productive, creative, and synergistic. This book will show you the way to create a home that is happy and healthy, in order for you to live a happy, healthy, wealthy life.

Imagine waking up feeling connected to your home and excited about your life. Imagine life in a Feng Shui-ed house.

This book is a beginner's guide to creating the life you want; a happy, healthy, wealthy life, learning about Feng Shui, and having fun along the way.

Sometimes you may not see the connection between what I'm teaching in this book and the practice of Feng Shui. You may wonder: *What does this have to do with Feng Shui? Is this even Feng Shui?* I ask that you trust the process because even when you start with just a few introductory practices, Feng Shui is incredibly powerful.

The aim of this book is for you to have an easy-to-implement overview of how Feng Shui can impact your home and life. It's the starting point as there are many layers to Feng Shui that I couldn't include here. I will show you how you can start putting some of these ideas into practice. I am known for making Feng Shui simple and actionable, and I want you to experience the magic that your home can be.

The Happy Home is made up of four parts that take you through the simple Feng Shui techniques and how they can support your personal and professional life.

Part One is all about the power of Feng Shui. You'll get the lowdown on its four thousand years old history and why it still exists today. You will start sending out powerful intentions for your home and begin to perceive it as you would a friend and as a relationship to nurture. You will take stock of where your relationship with your home is now, and how you have been treating it. You will learn how Feng Shui relates to energy and how this impacts your life. After all, your home has a soul, so being in conversation and connection with it is going to be crucial to changing your life.

Part Two looks at your home from a different viewpoint, releasing the negative memories that are holding you back and decluttering the physical obstacles to your happiness. This section also tackles letting go emotionally and energetically, as well as clearing the path to a better, brighter future.

In Part Three you'll get practical, learning to map your home from a classical Feng Shui perspective. We'll go through your home area by area, learning what each of the nine Power Centres represents and how to enhance each one with intention.

In Part Four, you'll learn some easy Feng Shui practices, before looking at your home room by room. We'll shine a spotlight on each room of the home from a Feng Shui angle so that you can be confident that what you add and take away will support the intentions you hold.

Finally, in Part Five, we will look at the personal aspects of Feng Shui with your personal trigram and power number, which has powerful benefits beyond the home. I'll also touch on your office, art and money, and auspicious Feng Shui subjects that we cannot overlook in a beginner's guide.

Throughout this book, I aim to bring clarity to your world and help you pave the way for success. The journey you are about to take will enable you to become fully aware of your current reality and where you are now, as well as introduce a new awareness that will allow you to open your eyes to possibilities you thought only happened to others. And all of this by embracing the power of Feng Shui through this book and making your home the happiest and most abundant it can be.

The Happy Home will allow you to start reaping the rewards of what you sow. It reveals how to create a home that complements your personal and professional goals. Whether you are looking to earn more money, get a new job, retire early, attract new clients, develop income streams, or enjoy more nurtured and better relationships, then this is the right book for you.

It's my intention to show you the power and simplicity of Feng Shui and how it can support your journey. To be crystal clear about what to expect, *The Happy Home* is about making the first commitment to learning about this practice. And if you have dabbled in Feng Shui before, or seen tips online, then this is the next step for you.

The Happy Home is where you'll learn the basics and become familiar with the energy of your home.

I like to describe Feng Shui as similar to an iceberg. At the top are the general tips you hear bandied around, like how you should keep your toilet seat down. The next layers are the different areas of your home and what they represent. After that comes how you set your furniture up for good Feng Shui. And at the very bottom are the invisible specific energies in your house that are either attracting or repelling what you want into your life. In this book, you'll learn the first few layers of Feng Shui and play with those.

Feng Shui has many elements and this book stops short of the personalisation that I teach in my signature programme, PowerHouse. For now, just sit back, relax, learn some Feng Shui basics, get comfortable with the energy of your home, and begin to understand it can support you. *The Happy Home* will take you as far as you can possibly go, without getting a personal home assessment through our programme.

One of the best things about Feng Shui is the incredible transformations I see and hear about in peoples' lives once they start to embrace this ancient art. As part of this book, I really wanted to highlight some of our incredible members who decided to embark on the journey of Feng Shui. Throughout the book, I have interwoven personal stories from women from all walks of life who stepped out of their comfort zones, implemented Feng Shui on all levels, and reaped powerful rewards and changes as a result.

These amazing PowerHouse members willingly and eagerly wanted to share their successes with you to inspire you to not just read this book and think *ohh that's very interesting* but to implement what I have shared with you. If it can happen for them, it can happen for you.

It's all good learning about how to set up your bedroom to attract love, but knowing and taking action are two totally different ball games. As I remind the participants of my signature PowerHouse course — *the word action is not in attraction for no reason.*

By the end of this book you will have an understanding of what Feng Shui is, how you can use it, and how you can turn your home into a happy, healthy, and wealthy space. You'll also learn about how your home is affecting your life, and what you can do to turn it around.

PART 1

The Power of Feng Shui

CHAPTER 1

My Story

I started my career as a holistic therapist, working with people and releasing stress and anxiety from their lives. I'm like Mary Poppins with a bag of powerful tools and modalities, from sound healing to yoga. Doing this inner and outer work, I came back to Feng Shui, a practice I had started when I was fifteen, but only used at home for myself. This book (and my work in this area as a whole) brings together all I learned in my time as a therapist and shares with you a unique perspective on Feng Shui.

I finally realised that it wasn't just about your own personal energy, or your mindset, but that your physical environment also had an impact on your life.

It's either sabotaging or supporting you.

Easy to implement

Your life starts at home. You spend hours a day in your house. You eat there, you sleep there, you cook there, you spend time with your family there. Your home is such an important part of your life, a place to kick off your shoes and settle in.

It's where you kiss, argue, and make up again. Everything that goes on inside the four walls of your home makes this practice and this book absolutely crucial. Your home is the foundation of everything. When it's out of whack, so is the rest of your life.

The purpose of this book is to release what is holding you back, connect with the energy of your home, clarify what you want to create and align your home with that energy. To become best friends with it. This book will help make your home the happiest and most abundant it can be.

When I talk about Feng Shui, I want to be crystal clear. Although it is all about the energy of your home, this book is packed with tangible, practical changes, so that you can be hands-on. You are about to become a powerful creator of your own happy, healthy, wealthy home using all these tools.

Give yourself the time to focus on the information and implement it. It will make it so much easier to absorb if you decide to put aside dedicated time each week.

You are here for a reason. Maybe you've experienced personal and professional challenges. Maybe you want to get unstuck. Maybe you've tried all sorts of things and are still not earning the money you desire or welcoming the love you long for. Maybe you have an interest in Feng Shui already. Whatever the reason, you've discovered Feng Shui and picked up this book. You're ready for more, so give it the time it deserves. Go at your own pace. And remember, you're in the right place.

I would recommend getting yourself a dedicated 'Feng Shui Journal' or notebook to document your journey and complete some of the exercises.

My vision for you

The vision I hold for you, the readers of this book, is to bring your home into the light. I see you bringing your home from a place of possible neglect or naivety, through the darkness, to love. Through doing so your life will flourish, just like the lotus flower.

If you're stuck in an infinite loop of personal and professional challenges, despite doing huge amounts of inner work to move on, you're in the right place. Finding the real problem is simple. You just haven't activated the hidden energy within your own home to make it flourish.

Using the power of Feng Shui, you can create radical changes in your income, career, and love. You can balance your home's energy, find more flow, and create a space that supports your dreams. Imagine how your life would look if you were receiving clients, love, opportunities, and blessings each and every day. Once you know the exact steps to take, your home has the power to do this for you. And this is exactly what I am going to walk you through.

Devour this book and you'll be able to use Feng Shui to turn your home into a happy and nurturing environment that supports your vision.

Honour your calling

Before we start, I have one last word of preparation. You are here for a reason. Honour the calling that you had to move forward and pick up this book.

With Feng Shui, believe me, some people will judge you. I can tell you from experience, that there will be people saying, "What are you doing? Why are you doing this? Who does Feng Shui? It's a bit out there, isn't it?"

Keep moving forward. It's not some kind of crazy superstition. It's real, it's powerful, and it's all for you. You don't even need to share it if you don't want to. When the whole world starts asking, "What's happened to you? Why is everything going your way at the moment?

You're in a great mood. Looks like you've been lucky lately." That's when to share your Feng Shui journey.

And still, people will judge, but that's on them! You don't have to believe in Feng Shui for it to work for you, but I feel like you're a believer. If you've read this far and you're here with me, it's time to do your thing and leave the rest. You don't have to push anyone else in your home into doing it either. (They will start to feel the changes anyway!) All you need to do is honour this calling yourself.

So, are you ready to make a huge and epic difference in your life? A balanced, harmonious, and happy home leads to a balanced, harmonious, and happy outer world. It's time to start creating your own happy, healthy, wealthy home.

Katie's Story

Katie is a naturopath from Australia who works from home. Before working with Feng Shui, she found that her home was really great for people but not so great for money. She felt like everything was just a bit of a struggle – brain fog, lacking motivation, and feeling like things were always in a trudge.

Katie became a member of our signature PowerHouse programme and began to implement Feng Shui remedies in her home. Like many of our members, she felt that she just had to dive right in and follow the guidelines of this ancient wisdom.

> *"I was freaking blown away. In my prosperity area, there was massive movement. It was like the shifting of an undercurrent. And once that settled down, I literally have had to keep a list of all the things that started to change.*
>
> *So, here is the list:*
>
> - *First of all, there was just a change in the energy of my home. It went from being a bit dull and brain foggy, to me feeling full of ideas for my business.*
> - *Also, I had a lot of uncomfortable feelings around my daughter becoming a teenager, but that all of a sudden became very harmonious.*
> - *There's been a huge shift of creativity flowing in relation to my business. After putting in my remedies, my business is exactly where I want it to be. I have the amount of clients that I want to see every week, and during the right times for me.*
> - *Out of the blue, I got the opportunity to MC a huge naturopathic conference.*

- **I am currently rolling out my own workshops, along with an Australia-wide tour. I'll be going to six different cities this year with it!**
- **Every time I put out a link or offer, I get people who want to join me.**
- **My husband's business started to see a substantial spike in revenue.**
- **On top of all this, we've paid down our mortgage, purchased an investment property, and we're now building an AirBnB!**

There has been a total energy shift."

CHAPTER 2

Introduction to Feng Shui

The most complicated part about Feng Shui is the pronunciation — FUNG SHWEE. But it doesn't really matter how you pronounce it, the most important part is embracing it into your life!

Let's begin with a question I'm sure you've asked yourself at some stage. Is Feng Shui just some kind of crazy superstition? Go on, admit it! It's crossed your mind, hasn't it? Maybe you've even dabbled a bit and encountered judgement from other people who think Feng Shui sounds a bit strange. That's why we're going to start by clearing up a few myths about what it is, and what it's not, giving you a little background on Feng Shui, where it comes from, why we use it, and what it can do for you.

What is Feng Shui?

Feng Shui is all about energy, or *chi*. In essence, you can think of Feng Shui as acupuncture for your home. It's a way of keeping the energy flowing in and around your home. The practice of Feng Shui is about making that energy as positive as possible, aligning your home for the highest good for you, your life, your business, your relationships, your opportunities, and the home itself. Originating in China, it uses the same Five Elements theories (Fire, Water, Earth, Metal, and Wood) as Traditional Chinese Medicine, Tai Chi, Qi Gong, and the Five Element Theory itself.

Feng Shui is a complex practice with many layers. There are also different schools of Feng Shui, but going into each and every one of those layers and schools is not within the scope of this book. For the purposes of *The Happy Home*, we are looking at the layers of Feng Shui that can bring you to a beautiful place with your home and a good level of understanding. To do so, we'll look at the layers of Feng Shui that use compass directions.

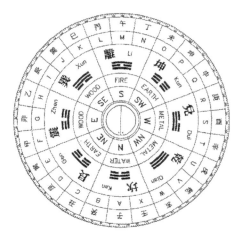

Loupan Compass

As a Feng Shui consultant, I use the traditional *Luo pan compass* in the PowerHouse programme which, as you can see, is highly technical. However, we won't be going into such complex layers in this book. We're still using the compass as a mapping tool for your home, just a much simpler one. Later, you will learn how to use the compass directions to map your home and find all of the corresponding life areas so that you can make them more supportive in your life.

Feng Shui may be complex, but this is for a good reason. In China, where Feng Shui originated, the first houses to be built according to Feng Shui were *built with intention*. That was four thousand years ago when Feng Shui was brought into its first form. In those times, people took into consideration where the sun rose, where the sun set, the situation or positioning of the home, and the land around it. Home-building was intentional. In fact, everything was done with powerful intention. What Feng Shui did was to bring that intention into people's environments, and into their homes.

The intention is the most important aspect of Feng Shui because it seems to me that intention has been lost in the world to a large degree. If you look at the way we create homes now, we just knock up houses anywhere. That is reflected in our lives too. Living with intention has shifted a great deal since the times when Feng Shui first came about.

What is Feng Shui for?

The purpose of Feng Shui, when the ancient Chinese first built those houses with intention, was for good health and a good harvest. And isn't that what we all want in the end? We want to be healthy and vibrant. We want everyone in our home to be happy. We also want a 'good harvest'. Back then, agriculture was the measure of prosperity; whatever the farmers sowed was harvested and became their abundance. Today, a good harvest is measured in whatever way you choose.

All in all, Feng Shui tunes into and honours the intentions you can set from within your home, using the energy in the most powerful ways. Feng Shui helps you create a space where you can feel more confident, supported, and empowered in your home, your life, and your business. Feng Shui exists to feel positivity; to harmonise interactions between the people in the home and between those in your life, to reduce arguments and disagreements, and to create a solid foundation. To flourish.

Feng Shui can influence a number of areas in your life, allowing you to spend time with and analyse each one. As you spend time with a particular life area, you may notice how it's mirrored by the energy in that part of your home.

Feng Shui is also oh-so subtle, making it important to trust the process and not rush through. It's not about immediate results, though they can happen. As the energy shifts in your home, it allows your space to become more magnetic to joy, love, pleasure, abundance, and success for you and everybody else living there. It breaks old patterns of lack and draws in the energy of abundance.

Does it work?

If these claims sound unbelievable to you, I get it. (I'm a Feng Shui consultant, so I'm biassed after all!)

But you don't just have to take my word for it. I'll let you into a little secret. An increasing number of successful people and organisations are investing in Feng Shui. This includes many large corporations, global entrepreneurs, hotels, banks, Hollywood directors, movie stars, TV presenters, and more.

To be specific, these are just a few of the names you might recognise that spend time, effort, and money on Feng Shui: Oprah, Shangri-La Hotel, Bank of America, Hyundai, and Whole Foods. They all use Feng Shui. Why? Because they are the kinds of people and organisations that use whatever they can to make their lives and businesses better and more successful. That's what you are doing here too and you're in good company. The sheer number of people using it should give you some comfort, but that's not all.

Feng Shui has long been the object of scorn for people who are dubious or sceptical of what we are doing here.

All I can do when people tell me that Feng Shui is "new-age hippie rubbish" is to laugh. Feng Shui is ancient. It's so old that it's being reignited for the modern world. By using Feng Shui in your life today, you are tapping into an ancient practice.

We will harness this ancient power, a power that can, and should, be available for everybody today. Everybody deserves to have a home that is supportive of their happiness, health, and wealth. So yes, it may be complex, but Feng Shui gets amazing results, and the rest of this book will attempt to make Feng Shui easy for you to implement to make your home feel good.

Your home remembers

Did you know that your house sees, hears, and feels everything that goes on inside it? Not only that, but your home has a memory. It remembers all the happy times, the sad times, the angry times, the past owner's stories, everything. It takes in all the emotions and witnesses all the goings-on. This directly affects your experience of your home. It directly affected everyone before you with everything that had gone on before them, and it is having a direct effect on what's happening in your life today.

Your home is also a dense physical manifestation. It is solid. It is fixed in place with bricks and mortar. It is not going anywhere. When energy comes in — whether happy, sad, angry or something else — it stays unless you allow it to be released. It is important that you move this negative energy out and make space for your desires and intentions to come forth. For your home to be a fertile place for amazing relationships, incredible abundance, joyous success, and happy families; old memories must be cleared.

Your home is a mirror of you and your unconscious. You are a mirror of your home. So, to begin your Feng Shui journey, you must start by treating your home like a person and cultivating a beautiful relationship with it. This begins by clearing your home of negative associations with the past.

Anatomy of your home

If you are going to create a friendship with your home, you must imagine it as a friend. Think of your friends for a moment. Each one has their own qualities, as well as their own flaws. Your home is just the same. It has its own personality, its own energy, and its own persona; from hearing, seeing, and feeling everything that has gone on inside it. This makes it interesting and unique. But just like any relationship, it can become strained.

If your house isn't your friend or if it has been your foe in the past, the likely conclusion is that it would not be supportive of you in your life. Why would your foe support you? Why would someone who has been disrespected help you to achieve great things? Likewise, why would a home that hasn't been looked after be a harmonious space for you to live in? Why would a place full of broken stuff treat you well? If the relationship between you both is tainted or stressed, you can only expect more negativity. But if you create a friendly relationship with your home, the opposite is true. It can be a powerful ally in your life. So, thinking about your house as a person — is your home a friend or foe?

It's not only in its ability to relate and support you that your home is like a person. Metaphorically, you can understand your home being like a person, with eyes, ears, and a mouth. The windows are your home's energetic eyes, 'the windows to the soul', bringing clarity to the inside from the outside. The walls are your home's energetic ears, hearing everything, soaking up every conversation, every argument, every party, everything. The front door is your home's energetic mouth.

Can you imagine functioning without your eyes, ears, or mouth? Difficult, right? If you don't look after those parts of your body, you would struggle to communicate or progress or nourish yourself. If you don't look after those corresponding parts of your home, guess what? It's difficult to see, hear, speak, and eat. In fact, it would be hard to live any kind of life of abundance, joy, or happiness if you were not clear on where you were going and creating the nourishing conditions for it to happen.

Your home sees

First, let's look at your home's eyes — the windows — to see what this means in practice. If your eyes are somehow blocked, you can't see what's coming for you or where you're going. By clearing the eyes, literally cleaning the windows of your home and removing the dirt that obscures your view, you receive more clarity about your life. You are able to see what's coming. You can find your way again, instead of being lost or confused. And you will avoid hurting yourself or getting injured.

EXERCISE: See clearly

1. Clean the windows of your home. Repeat the affirmation, "I can see clearly where I am going and what is coming to me."

Your home hears

Next, let's look at the ears — the walls — and clear away the negativity. The walls have contained all the words ever spoken within your home, all the stories of the past. Just like your ears hear what you and others say, the walls of your home have heard the arguments, the conversations, the upsets, the secrets, and the broken promises. The walls remember those moments and the emotions held within old stories. That energy is still housed within the walls of your home, still impacting you and your life. To let go of everything it has heard, you must flush the negative memories out of the home.

EXERCISE: Release past stories

1. Take your journal and write out all the memories and past stories you have from being in your home. Anything that comes up that you want to release, write it down. Anything that you remember as a particularly happy moment, write that down as well. And anything that you know about the previous owners or residents in the house, write that down too. If you don't know of any traumatic experiences that went on in your house before you lived there, just write down what you do know from your time there.

   Here are some prompts to help the memories flow:

   - Anything traumatic
   - Anything emotional
   - Anything that caused anxiety or stress
   - Interactions with neighbours
   - Interactions with friends
   - Interactions with family
   - Interactions with your partner
   - Arguments
   - Something breaking
   - Something upsetting you
   - Times you upset someone else
   - Times you received bad news
   - Stories or rumours about past owners

2. Try not to overthink this writing process. Allow the memories to come up and flow out onto the paper without judgement. If it's a memory within you, it is a memory still in the walls of your house that needs to be released. By committing it to paper, you begin to release the memory from your energy system.

Note: This process will have an impact on your energy system, the energy systems of everybody who lives in your home, and the energy system of your home itself. While your home will become your best friend by releasing all these memories in the long run, this process can leave you depleted in the short term. You may feel tired after doing this part of the exercise. You may also feel huge resistance to sitting down and doing it. If either of these is the case, know that it is completely natural. Be gentle with yourself. Take a break. Sit outside and take a few breaths or go out for a walk, then come back to it.

3. Once you have your list, go through the negative memories one by one and consciously decide to let go of each one. To do this, look at the memory and ask aloud, "Do I want to let go of this?" Then answer aloud, "Yes, I do." Alternatively, you can ask yourself, "Am I ready to release this memory now?" And you would respond, "Yes, I am ready to release this now."

Note: If you think your partner or family may think you're a bit strange for doing this ritual, try to do it when you have time to yourself.

4. Once you have gone through each and every one of the memories, put them into a small fire-proof container and burn the pages. Please take care doing this and make sure you stay safe. I recommend doing this outside if you can or throwing the pages into a lit fireplace if you have one. If not, I suggest a metal dish for burning the pages, then washing the ashes down the sink or toilet with running water.

As you burn the negative memories, you honour your house by completely letting go of all that has been held inside your energy system and the energy system of your home. If you can't do any of these, visualise the release of bad memories from your home. If it's not safe to burn them, just tear them up and put them in the bin.

With the physical release of the ashes of those burned pages, you may feel an emotional release. If you feel the need to cry when anything comes up, it's okay to shed some tears. Remember, you may have been holding this inside of you for quite some time. You may really want to get rid of these memories quickly, but be gentle with yourself. Afterwards, I recommend going out into the fresh air, even going out barefoot onto some grass if you can, taking some more deep breaths, going for a walk, and allowing yourself to feel cleared of the past. Drink plenty of water to flush all the emotions out of your body too.

If some of the memories are still lingering, download my 'letting go' audio from: ***www.patricialohan.com/***

happyhomebonuses or read the guided meditation here, and do it for yourself.

Get yourself into a nice, comfortable position on a chair.

Make yourself feel as cosy as you possibly can.

Give yourself permission to take this time out from your day, from all of the experiences going on in your life. Affirm and know that everything is working perfectly and that it is safe for you to take this time out of your day to check-in and drop into a safe space of deep relaxation.

Watching your breath come in and out — in and out.

Slowing it down.

Drop into a safe space of relaxation.

With each exhale, allow yourself to go deeper and deeper and deeper into relaxation.

Take a moment now to scan your body from the crown of your head for any tension. Scan down over your face, your jaw, your neck, and your shoulders. Allow the tension to just melt away. Continue to scan down your arms and your hands, your shoulder blades, your spine, your diaphragm, all of your internal organs, all the way down into your hips, your pubic bone, your thighs, your knees, your ankles, and your feet. As you do so, feel totally relaxed. Go deeper and deeper into relaxation.

Now watch the rise and fall of your breath, the gentle rise and fall of your breath. And realise with every inhale the capacity to breathe out is part of the natural life cycle. The inhale is an opportunity to breathe new, fresh, positive, powerful breath into your body, to rejuvenate your cells. And the exhale is an opportunity to let go of any thoughts, worries, or things that no longer serve you. This natural cycle of inhaling and exhaling is how we breathe and how our body moves and brings fresh, new oxygen into our body and cells every day. Notice that if you don't exhale, you cannot inhale and bring new energy and fresh air into your body.

Now notice your capacity to inhale and your capacity to exhale. There is an abundance of fresh air available for you to breathe in at all times. It is safe to exhale and let go after each and every inhale. This is the cycle of life, inhaling, breathing in the new, exhaling, breathing out and letting go of the old to make space for more of the new. Watch this cycle for a few more breaths and just notice if you can balance the inhale with the exhale.

Now bring your awareness back into the body and allow yourself to bring items or things in your home that you feel a resistance to let go of into your mind's eye. See these items in front of you, one or maybe several things, and just notice between you and these items, the cords, the energetic cords that appear between you and them. You may be able to feel the cords, they could look like ropes or chains, some of them very tightly connected and others very loose, maybe like wool, the thread between you and them. The connections could be coming from any part of you to any part of the item. And these threads, or cords, or cables, represent the powerful connection between you and them. And these could be very heavy things that could be holding you back from really moving forward in your life because of these strong connections and ties that you've created energetically.

Now it is time to give yourself permission to release and let go of any of these cords and cables that may no longer serve you because, as you release these cords and cut them, these items are no longer energetically connected to you. By releasing them and letting them go, you are making space to welcome fresh new energy into your life. Just like the inhale and the exhale. In your mind's eye, I want you to imagine in your right hand, the perfect cutting implement that comes into your hand. This could be scissors, a saw, or a knife, that is absolutely perfect for cutting the cords between you and the items that you are now ready to let go of. Holding this cutting implement in your hand, look at the items and thank them. Thank them for the memories which you will never forget. Thank them for the experience of having them in your possession and realise that it is now safe to let them go so that you are welcoming brand new, fresh items into your life that spark joy and feel good.

Now use that perfect tool to cut through these cords. Some of them may be really flimsy and just cut and melt away almost instantly. Others could take much longer and be much more difficult, but connect with the energy of knowing that by letting go of the item, you are making space to welcome in new energy. Just like the cycle of our breath. And with an exhale, letting go, letting go, letting go, letting go, letting go, letting go. See the cords and cables now melt into the ground and disappear. You are no longer connected to these items and it is now safe for you to let go of them and welcome brand new, fabulous items into your life.

Take a nice deep breath in now, and exhale, letting go. Bring your awareness back into your body, back into your breath, wiggle your fingers and your toes, and bring the energy back into every cell of your body. Feel yourself stretch out, stretch, stretch, stretch, stretch, stretch, stretch, stretch, stretch, stretch. Feel yourself lighter, brighter, and more at ease, to welcome all the good into your life now.

Your home nourishes

Lastly, let's look at the mouth of your home — the front door. This is the main door you come in through, and it doesn't matter if it is at the side of the house. It controls what goes into your body to be processed. It's where food goes in, money goes in, and energy goes in. Everything flows in through your front door.

The entrance is a vital aspect of your home and you need to become conscious of what is going in the front door if you are going to build a happy and supportive relationship. Building any friendship means respecting and honouring the home and its energy, which means being incredibly mindful of how you nourish the space and what gets in.

One of the most important aspects of front doors is that you must use them! Imagine if you were in a relationship with someone who never spoke, was unable to communicate, and didn't look after themselves by having healthy food. It would be almost impossible. It's about looking after yourself. It's how you get fed. It's how energy gets in. So, start going in through the front door. In some cultures, particularly in Ireland where I'm from, it's a big deal for people to use the front door and they always use the back door. For Feng Shui, this is so significant and using the front door is where you can start making a real difference (even just using it once a day will help feed your house).

Another aspect of the front door is to open it up. If you are able to be near the door or you are in the garden outside, keep it open for a short while, allowing it to be open and feeling the energy coming in. This is a way of feeding your home.

Lastly, if you were inviting a guest to your home, you'd want to start the relationship with a good first impression, making them feel welcome. And your home is like a friend, remember? So, make your front entrance beautiful, with a gorgeous front door, keeping it nice and clean, adding flowers and a welcome mat to make it look inviting. Isn't that going to welcome more positive energy? It is bound to!

EXERCISE: Open up

1. Start using your front door as much as possible. If you are at home and able to be around the front door, keep it open for a while.
2. Clean the front door and sort out the entrance area. Use the affirmation, "I welcome good things into my life now." Spend some time with it.

Note: You don't want dead plants, cobwebs, or broken items around the entrance, nor a doorbell that doesn't work. All of that pushes energy away. It's like standing at the front door saying, "We don't want you in here. We want to starve." If you don't feed your home, the *energy* of the house is starving.

3. Ensure your front door is easy to open. When it is open, welcome in the chi by saying aloud, "Come on in, good energy. You're welcome."

If the door is difficult to open, or you have to fight to open it or turn the key, it is hard to bring the energy in. This represents life feeling like a struggle.

Over the course of this chapter, you'll have noticed a lot of clearing away of old stagnant negative energy to welcome in the new. Sometimes we have to go into the darkness to allow in the light. That's what clearing is all about. Do not underestimate the power of releasing stories from your home or opening up for good energy to come in. And do not imagine that you can do these practices once and expect to be done. There will be layers and layers of memories and stories to let go of. You will clean and clear entryways over and over again.

For now, though, congratulate yourself on a job well done. It's not easy to go into the dark but you've done it. Now it's time to let in some light; to take a closer look at the relationship you're in with your home, and start thinking about the good intentions that you want to welcome and allow.

CHAPTER 3

Assessing Your Relationship with Your Home

Every single day, you spend hours and hours in your home. You sleep in it for a start, so you are there for at least six to eight hours, maybe more. You could be someone who works from home or, for some other reason, spends twenty-plus hours inside the home each day, only going out for a little while. That's a lot of time to be in one space. It's a big commitment to a building!

As we touched on in the last chapter, you are in a relationship with your home. We've dealt with the idea of having a negative or unsupportive relationship between you, and started to transform your home from foe into a friend. In this chapter, you will begin to realise the connection between you and the place where you're living now and discover more about that relationship. You want to know as much as you can about that connection if you are going to spend so much time there because it's important you get along well.

Going back to your friendships, you may know someone who you love spending time with. If you're great friends and you get along well, you want to spend a lot of time together. On the other hand, maybe there are people in your life who you avoid and don't want to spend any time with at all. You do everything you can to avoid them. And if you do have to spend time with those people, you're not going to be happy about it. Imagine if you had to spend over twenty hours every day with someone. You'd want that person to be one of the people you like, right? One of those people you want to spend time with. Your home is exactly the same. You want it to be in that 'best friends' category.

Here's what a friendship with your home is not:

- Taking it for granted
- Allowing it to be used and abused
- Never loving or nurturing it
- Only sleeping there
- Coming and going but not spending time there
- Banging doors
- Not tidying up
- Not keeping it clean
- Leaving appliances on
- Letting furniture get shabby
- Ignoring items that are broken
- Leaving anything in a state of disrepair

When you mistreat your home in this way, but you're constantly in that space, the energy of neglect in that friendship is affecting you, your productivity, your sleep, your prosperity, and your family relationships.

Ensuring a friendship with your home (or maintaining that friendship, if you are already friends) means there's always space for improvement and growth. Friendships take time, commitment, and energy. And they are oh-so worthwhile when you invest in them fully. Having a friend is a gift and a joy.

Most important of all when it comes to friendships is knowing where you stand. Isn't it much easier to get along with people who are open and transparent? Let's assess your relationship with your home so that you know where you're starting from and how to go from strength to strength.

EXERCISE: How do you and your home get along?

1. Answer these questions 'yes' or 'no'. There are no right or wrong answers. This is simply a tool for assessing your relationship, so you know where you're starting from and what you can improve. The more honest you can be with yourself, the better understanding you will have about how to move forward.

    Q1. Do you feel happy when you think of your home? Y/N

    Q2. Have things improved in your life since you moved in? Y/N

Q3. Have your finances improved in this home? Y/N

Q4. Is it easy to relax in your home? Y/N

Q5. Do people like to visit and stay at your home? Y/N

Q6. Do you sleep well in your home? Y/N

Q7. Do people compliment the energy of your home? Y/N

2. Read the assessments below and reflect in your journal.

MOSTLY YESES: *What a great start! Your home is your friend and you're already getting along well. Like any friendship, there is always room for improvement. Remember it takes time and energy to maintain that relationship. You are already on track. See what unfolds as you strengthen this bond!*

MOSTLY NOES: *Even though your home is more foe than a friend right now, awareness is key. And now you have that. When creating any good relationship, it's important to know where you're starting out from. Maybe you're not getting along that well right now, but the best part is you can turn it around from here!*

The core purpose of Feng Shui is to build a strong, powerful connection with your home. After the investigation and cleansing you have already started in your space, you have set up the foundation for a solid relationship later on. In the next chapter, you'll take the first step towards that loving, nurturing, supportive connection.

CHAPTER 4

Connecting with the Heart of Your Home

By releasing and freeing yourself and your home of its past stories, cleansing, and clearing the openings to your house so that you can see a clear direction and invite in good energy, you have created space for new positive loving memories to be welcomed in. You have a clean slate on which to start writing your future friendship, a happy, and mutually beneficial relationship. By clearing as you have in the previous chapters, you have made space inside you. Nature abhors a vacuum, so it is time to start thinking about what kind of friendship will move into that space.

To make any kind of meaningful connection with a friend, you need to connect heart-to-heart, soul-to-soul. In the earlier chapter on your home being like a person who can hear, see, and speak, we looked at the ears, eyes, and mouth of your home. Yet a person feels in their heart. If you are going to create amazing energy that's

100% supportive of your life, you'll need a home with a huge heart.

Growing the love between you starts by cultivating gratitude for your home and telling your home all about the amazing memories that you intend to make within it. Now that you have this new connection and are setting out to be best friends with your home, you are going to start making positive stories and memories together.

As you have freed yourself of the past, the old stories you were holding onto have evaporated. So what stories do you want to replace those with now that the old ones are gone? What do you want to create from here on?

I suggest writing them into being with a **love letter** to your home, telling it everything you wish to happen. This is your opportunity to ask your home, in pure gratitude, from a place of deep love, for the supportive friendship you desire.

By creating this energetic connection between you and the soul of your home, you are opening the lines of communication. Your house even has the capacity to provide a remedy for any ills you have right now and is able to give you feedback, information, and insights into better living.

EXERCISE: Love letter

1. Look back at and reflect on the happy memories from the exercise in the earlier chapter on

clearing your home of the past. Ask yourself what other happy memories you want to welcome in. Express gratitude for all the positive memories. Express forgiveness for all those negative ones that you let go of. Acknowledge the space you've created and now want to fill.

2. Find a pen and paper, and write down what you want to create for yourself, your family, and everyone who lives in, and comes to, your home. Write these wishes in the style of a love letter to your home. Elaborate on the memories you intend to create there. Use your imagination. State what you want to create. Write the letter in the present tense and fill it with gratitude for this future coming into being.

To get you started, take a look at this example.

Dear Home,

I am grateful for the shelter you have provided for me. I am excited to create a new friendship with you. I am so happy to open the door every day when I come home from work and to know you are waiting. I love how much fun I have here now and how my family is so harmonious. We have fabulous visitors and dinner parties with wonderful friends.

Thank you! Love, Patricia xxx

Once you have declared your desires, it's time to really connect with them. You have opened the channels. You are now sitting in a powerfully creative space, putting down strong roots for your home and your life. Taking the intentions you have written in the love letter to your home.

Give yourself some space to do the Soul Of Your Home Meditation. The script is below or you can download a recording of it with the powerful Tibetan bowls in the background from here:

www.patricialohan.com/happyhomebonuses

Sarah's Story

Sarah is an actress, film director, screenwriter, and an online coach for artists.

She had always been intrigued by Feng Shui but found dealing with the compass points complicated. She'd just moved into a new apartment and had a feeling it would be good for her.

Did she still find it too complicated to do?

> *"No, Patricia made the process very easy because I don't like getting overwhelmed with mathematics and calculations, and she broke it down very, very easily, and told me exactly*

what to do. She was there every step of the way, and then I gave her my information, and I waited and was so excited, and then we had another call where she was explained each section of my house, what it represented, and what I needed to do to Feng Shui it, and it was really simple and it didn't require moving around any furniture, which I was really freaking out about. It just required putting down certain simple everyday things that were easily found.

Then Patricia did this meditation where she linked me to the house. Now, no word of a lie, that night the house started speaking to me. I was like, 'The house is speaking to me!' I can't even remember what it said, but it was very profound and, since that day, I almost feel like I'm in tune with the house."

The most profound thing for Sarah was when she dealt with the career area and started to get incredible jobs out of the blue.

After seeing how much it helped Sarah and her family improve their lives, Sarah plans to Feng Shui a new house they've bought, and cannot imagine life now without Feng Shui.

But does she think it will work for people who don't believe it will?

"It will work. It's all about harmony. It's all about creating balance and harmony in your private space because if you feel at home in your home, and you feel calm, you're open to receiving all the amazing things coming to you. So, that's all it is! It's just creating energetic balance in your home, and if you feel calm you're open to receiving all the amazing things coming to you. It's just about creating an energetic balance in your home, with remedies. And the remedies are everyday things."

Meditation to connect with the Soul of Your Home

This meditation will allow you to truly connect with the vision you hold for yourself, for your future, for your life in that home, for your family, for your friends, for the activities you want to do in that home, and for receiving success and abundance in your life.

Get yourself into a comfortable position, whether it's sitting down somewhere or lying on your bed. Adjust yourself so your shoulders are relaxed, and your body feels fully relaxed and settled. Come into the space, into your breath, and into your body. Let go of the day, let go of any thoughts floating across your mind, and just come into the breath. Give yourself permission to relax completely.

Allow yourself to get even more relaxed. Mentally repeat, "My muscles are melting. My muscles are melting."

And in this relaxed space, we're going to connect with the heavens above, the universal life force energy, and the Mother Creator, the heart of Mother Earth. So, imagine a beautiful beam of light coming from the heavens. This beam of light is glowing down onto the crown of your head, onto the crown chakra. And this light that's flooding down, this unlimited supply of beautiful light is beaming down, washing over your body, cleansing, healing, clearing, and releasing anything that is in not alignment with this high vibrational, powerful love energy.

Allow the light now to filter down through the crown chakra behind the third eye. Relax the forehead. Behind the eyes, the eye relaxes. The nose, the jowls, the cheeks. Allow that light to flood through, all the way down to the neck, cleansing the throat chakra. Down.

As you feel the shoulders relax, release any tension across the shoulders, as your entire body has now been illuminated by this powerful energy.

Flooding down the central channel, along the spine now, cleansing the heart chakra, down into the solar plexus. Allow this light to flood into the lungs, and the chest. It's completely illuminated. All the way down into the solar plexus. All the organs are filled with this beautiful, loving light. The light beams down both arms, and out through the fingertips. It illuminates and cleanses any darkness.

Now, move down into the sacral chakra. The entire central channel and the entire body have now been filled. All the organs are illuminated and cleansed. The light pours down, down, down, down, down into the root chakra, and down the legs, all the way down through the hips, the legs, the knees, the ankles, the feet. This energy moves down through the feet, all the way into Mother Earth.

As it breaks through the soil, it moves down, down, down, down through the layers in the earth, all the way down, down, down, down, down, down, down right into the centre of the earth, right into the middle heartbeat of the earth. We come to this fire energy, the colour of the root chakra, the centre of Mother Earth. And that white light that's pouring all the way down through us beams, and now wraps around the core of the earth, Mother Gaia, where all is made manifest and brought to reality from this centre of the earth.

And now, this red energy, this colour of passion and fire element, starts to move all the way back up, up, up, up, up, up, up, up, up, up, up, up, up, up through the channel created, all the way up to the feet, through the legs, all the way up, bringing this fire energy from Mother Earth all the way up, up, up, up, up, up, up. An infinite supply of fire energy comes all the way up until it reaches the heart chakra.

And these two lights ... this fire energy comes at one with the heart, with the white light from the heavens. And these two colours start to mingle together, like mixing a paint can, the fire, and the white. It's creating this beautiful synergy of red and white, this gorgeous colour of pink, the colour of unconditional love, pure love.

And as these two energies come together, with you right at the heart of it, your entire body now starts to permeate this energy of unconditional love. You are fully aligned with this energy of unconditional love, pure unconditional love. Allowing this energy now to fill up your entire body, your entire auric field. There's a bubble of pink energy all around you.

And from this space of unconditional love, I want you to drop into your heart, and connect with your intention for your home. The intentions of love, joy, peace, happiness, abundance, success, ease, and flow. All of these words are for your intention, for you and your home. And knowing there's an infinite supply of this energy from the heavens and from Mother Earth.

From your heart, I want you to imagine this river of pink energy flooding out of your heart, infused with all of your intentions for your house, flowing out of your heart into the room that you're in now, into the furniture, into the walls, into the artwork. Allowing that energy to flood and flow from your heart into each and every cell of your home, into each and every nook and cranny, all the corners and crevices, into the cupboards, into the wardrobes, into all of the storage areas. Allowing this energy of unconditional love that's infused with your intentions for your home, the intentions of love, joy, fun, ease, abundance, and success flood your entire home.

And feel the energy of your home now absorbing these intentions. As you move through each and every room, feel the continuous flow from your heart moving into the bedrooms, and the kitchen, and the living room, the dining area, the bathrooms, the entrance, so the entire area is now filled with this powerful energy of unconditional love, infused with all of your powerful intentions. And allow yourself now to drop in any other words that you would like to see unfold, any other intentions that you have for your home. And like waves of energy from your heart, see it flowing and filling up your entire home with these energies.

And now, you've set this beautiful, loving energy into every single part of your home. Dropping back, and feeling that connection. Feeling your home absorbing these energies. Feeling it sighing, and going, "Oh, this is what you want? Mm, feels good." And while you're in this loving, deep connection with your home, you have this open space and these open lines of communication between you and the soul of your home. And I want you to take this opportunity to ask your home what it wants from you. What does it need to accomplish all of these intentions, and to provide you with all of these intentions? Maybe you'll hear something. Maybe you'll get a feeling. Maybe you'll get a sense of it. But just give yourself permission to allow whatever comes in to be just perfect.

And know that now that you have opened these lines of communication between you and your home like never, ever before. It's here, and it's listening, and it's so grateful for this powerful, infinite, loving energy that you have filled the space up with. Feel the gratitude of your home, and send gratitude to it for the shelter it provides for you. Let it know that things are going to change a little bit now with the energy of the home and that you are really excited about co-creating your intentions together with this beautiful home, and becoming friends that have so much fun and positive experiences together. Thank your home for this experience. Thank your home for listening.

Take a big, deep breath in, and absorb whatever it is that you need now. And now, bring your awareness back into the room, into your body, into your breath. And allow yourself to just enjoy these few moments of quiet, while you come back into this real life, and into your body. And assimilate all that you experienced. Know that any time that you feel inclined, you can just drop back into this meditation to connect again with the soul of your home, or just ask it because it's here now to support you, and to co-create your dreams with it.

In Part One, you thoroughly stripped away the past and began to familiarise yourself with the kind of relationship you need to have with your home in order for the practice of Feng Shui to make deep and long-lasting changes in your life. In Part Two, the intentions you have just set will begin to manifest into reality and the flow will get underway. You will start to physically and specifically make real changes to bring your powerful intentions into being.

PART 2

Feng Shui Flow

CHAPTER 5

Your Home with Different Eyes

Do you know the state your home is in? How about whether you're nourishing your home with goodness or draining it of potential? What's working and what's not when it comes to the happiness, health, and wealth that your home is attracting?

As you have before, imagine your home as a person. In order for her to be happy, healthy, and wealthy, would you feed her junk food every day, cheap economy food, or processed food? If that's what she was eating all day, every single day, she'd be pretty unhappy. She would not be healthy. And even though the food is unhealthy, she probably wouldn't feel all that wealthy either, eating out of a paper bag or wrapper, no plates or cutlery, plastic tables, and so on. Safe to say she wouldn't be happy, healthy, or wealthy living on a diet of rubbish.

The same goes for your home. Yet how do you know what 'diet' you're feeding your home? Well, in the same way you might keep a food diary for a while, you need to check in with the happiness, health, and wealth of your home in a practical way and note whether things are 'just okay', 'pretty good', or 'excellent'. It's time to take an inventory of your home!

Room for improvement

Taking stock of your home isn't about preparing for a huge expensive overhaul, but it does give you a starting point that you can analyse. You can see clearly the next upgrade you want to make. You can easily decide the next item you're going to bring in to improve your environment. The idea is you walk into your house and *feel* first-class, whatever that is for you.

Before we start, let me give you some examples of simple upgrades that have had a big impact. Several times over the last couple of years, my husband and I have made simple changes to our home that have made a huge difference in our lives. For example, we had this wooden couch that was terrible. We couldn't even sit on it without getting sore. One day, I turned around and said, "You know what? We're getting a new couch". The same day, we bought a beautiful, elegant, purple velvet couch. To us, it's stunning and 100% first class. To us, walking in the door, it's like, *wow!* Every time we sit on it, we love it. Every time someone comes to see us at home, they're stunned. All the time, we hear, "Oh my God, that couch is amazing!" Upgrading our couch — one simple change — made a massive impact on the way we felt in our home. It sparked so much joy and so much comfort.

Sometimes we think that upgrades need to be super expensive, but they don't. Another example I have is from a client who pimped her bathroom, which was her prosperity area. When she realised it represented prosperity in her home, but was really shabby and taken for granted, she bought fluffy new towels, bathroom mats, beautiful incense, gorgeous soap, and put some flowers in there. Her attitude was, *I'm going to make this a luxury bathroom.* Imagine the difference that made to the way she felt.

Let's look at the alternative scenario. Say your bathroom mirror was cracked. That's not a first-class experience. When you look in the mirror at the crack, that projects back at you. Every day, it's depleting your energy and the energy of that space. Yet a mirror is easily replaced, without having to spend a lot for the difference it makes to your life.

Classifying your home

That's why you need to take an inventory. So that you can see clearly where improvements can be made in every part of your home for the greatest impact on your life.

The idea is to classify the areas of your home by economy, business class, and first class, so you can see where it is already amazing and where there's an opportunity to improve. Let's take a look at those classifications:

Economy Class

It's fine, works okay, is functioning, or maybe it's a bit broken. It's just doing its job, but no more. You're just making do.

Business Class

It's a little plusher, feels better, is more exclusive, and is functioning well. You treated yourself a little bit better here. You've got a little bit more space.

First Class

It's the best you can buy, the exact one you want, the organic version, the healthiest and most positive version, the item that has a ripple effect of good energy for your home, the items that make you feel '*yes, I love it!*' You wouldn't change it no matter what. It doesn't necessarily have to be the most *expensive* thing, it's more about how it makes you *feel*.

EXERCISE: Taking an inventory

1. Starting at your front door, move around each area and feel into what you're keeping in your home that is **first class** (if you had all the money in the world, you would definitely still keep that item or room exactly as it is), **business class**

(good, but room for improvement), or **economy class** (not filling your home with joy or just making do).

2. Use the list below and mark which class the item belongs to at the moment. Look at each room for potential. See which class it fits into now. Then take your journal and write down any insights you have for where you can improve.

I have created an inventory checklist that you can download, to easily go through all areas of your home at: www.patricialohan.com/happyhomebonuses

As you go about this exercise, be gentle with yourself. It may not make you feel good, especially if you think, *oh my God, my whole house is economy class!* This exercise is about awareness, not judgement. It's about figuring out where you're at, so you can see where there is room for improvement. When you go gently, you get to look at each area without judging where you are or how you can afford to improve it. In short, it's about the *possibility* of your home. And that's exciting!

Here are a few ideas and questions to get you looking at your home from a new perspective:

Are you walking by something every single day and taking it for granted?

Are you struggling to get in the door of a room and just ignoring it?

Are there items that are broken?

What can you notice about the way your home feels in different areas?

What could you upgrade today?

As you walk around your home making notes, it's common to wonder, *what does this have to do with Feng Shui?* But it is so profound. The visible opportunities and long-term transformation you will see by the end are so powerful once you analyse your house from this viewpoint. Start taking action one tiny step at a time. Most importantly, don't beat yourself up, have fun, and enjoy the process.

Checklist

Front Entrance	Economy Class	Business Class	First Class
Front Door			
Door Handle			
Welcome Mat			
Plants			
Doorbell			
Entry Way			
Storage			
Name / Number			
First Impressions			
Hallway			
Flooring			
Artwork			

Paintwork			
Storage			
Overall Feel			
Living Room/ Family Room	**Economy Class**	**Business Class**	**First Class**
Couch			
Other furniture			
Flooring			
Artwork			
Paintwork			
Plants			
Curtains			
Cushions			
Overall Feel			
Kitchen			
Kitchen Table			
Chairs			
Cooker			
Fridge			
Artwork			
Flooring			
Paintwork			
Crockery			
Serving Dishes			
Pots and Pans			
Silverware			
Cooking Utensils			
Small Kitchen Appliances			
Knives			
Overall Feel			

Dining Room	Economy Class	Business Class	First Class
Artwork			
Dining Table			
Chairs			
Décor			
Flooring			
Storage			
Napkins			
Fruit Bowl			
Overall Feel			
Master Bedroom	Economy Class	Business Class	First Class
Mattress			
Headboard			
Storage			
Wardrobe			
Hangers			
Linen			
Duvet			
Pillows			
Throws			
Reading Lamps			
Side Tables			
Flooring			
Artwork			
Overall Feel			
Other Bedrooms	Economy Class	Business Class	First Class
Mattress			
Headboard			
Linen			
Storage			
Flooring			

Paintwork			
Side Tables			
Overall Feel			
Bathrooms / Toilets	**Economy Class**	**Business Class**	**First Class**
Artwork			
Paintwork			
Flooring			
Towels			
Bathroom Mat			
Soap			
Shower Power			
Storage			
Plants			
Overall Feel			
Other Rooms	**Economy Class**	**Business Class**	**First Class**
Pantry			
Laundry Room			
Closets			
Toy Room			
Conservatory			
Car Garage			
Outdoor Areas			
Outdoor Furniture			
Garden			
Lawns			
Flowers			

Important things to note about the checklist:

- If you see things that are one star, don't beat yourself up. Just know that there is so much more than you can enjoy from this part of your home!

- Take some time to look for the five-star version of some of these items. Get a sample of a plush, expensive carpet. Collect a photo example of your dream kitchen. Place these examples in the part of your home they are associated with.
- When you see it in your space, you will get excited and know the upgrade is on the way!

Mary's Story

Mary's passion is energy healing and she is a qualified clinical hypnotherapist.

She came to Feng Shui because she felt 'stuck'. She knew there was a lot of clutter in her house and had tried to declutter it herself just as another friend was starting my programme and recommended it to her.

Since decluttering she has found the freedom to start loving her home, after going through a four-year acrimonious and lengthy judicial separation, where she couldn't do anything with her house apart from keeping it clean and tidy. Since doing the PowerHouse course, Mary has replaced all internal door handles that were damaged by her children when they were younger, replaced the front door, and moved the location of a mirror.

These actions all represented her getting a grip on reality and a grip on life and her finances. They also made the house much more welcoming and positive.

Before she moved there, eleven years earlier, the house had seen many people renting or owning it for short periods. But after cleansing and implementing the remedies in the house, Andrea and her children became a lot happier and the home had a much nicer vibe.

She also saw a lot more clients coming in and just randomly choosing to get in touch with her. Money bonuses and gifts started coming her way too.

So, what would she tell people who are thinking about bringing Feng Shui into their lives?

> *"Definitely go for it! Definitely. It just makes perfect sense to me. It is acupuncture for your house, as you're getting the energy free-flowing. And even doing that report gives you light bulb moments: why your house is the way it is, why it's affecting the people in the house, or even outside the house, and how it can free flow everything. You just feel unstuck, and you're opening up a whole new world of more positivity for yourself. It's amazing.*
>
> *The people in my house, my kids, are happier. I'm happier. And I'm grabbing*

any opportunity that comes by now, putting myself out there, and just going for it.

Feng Shui has pushed me out of my comfort zone and I'm not going for anything and everything that's coming my way anymore.

It's the universe saying, "Hey! Here's another chance. Give this a go and see where this road brings you now." And I love that. I don't hesitate anymore. I just go for it. I don't even think about it. I just go for it. This is the right way."

Mary found she'd had a massive positive shift in her energy and in her life and luck generally.

CHAPTER 6

Making Space

It's one of my favourite words because I know how much juice there is in the act of making space. *It* opens the floodgates to a flow of happiness, health, and wealth entering your life and makes such a difference when you recognise the power in this process. So, what *is* the word?

declutter /diːˈklʌtə/ [*verb*]

to remove unnecessary items from (an untidy or overcrowded place)

In the last chapter, you looked at the opportunities for improvement in your home. So you've already started taking an inventory of the stuff you have and how it feels. But did you know that having too much stuff, having 'unnecessary items', and the overcrowding, the clutter, can hinder your happiness, health, and wealth? Time to look at the impact clutter is having on your life with some important questions.

What is clutter?

Clutter is the stuff that's making you stuck. It's the stuff you're holding on to, that you have a connection with on some emotional level, that is stopping you from moving forward. Clutter is not the everyday messiness of life. It's not the few clothes on the floor that you were wearing yesterday, so don't fool yourself into thinking you're decluttering just by tidying up. Clutter goes far deeper than that.

How is clutter impacting your life?

Honestly, clutter is causing stress and anxiety in your life, plain and simple. Having a lot of stuff around your house creates a lack of focus and clarity. It makes you feel stuck. It stops you from going places, literally, and metaphorically. It also wastes your time, because you can wander around looking for things for ages when your home isn't organised or when something is hidden with lots of other stuff.

Clutter prevents the flow of energy around your home, as I mentioned in Part One. Energy becomes blocked, stuck, and unable to move when you have lots of clutter, which means that energy is held up and not flowing around your home, bringing in all the good stuff.

If clutter is stopping the flow of energy and you want energy to flow, the answer seems simple, doesn't it? You need to declutter.

Why would you declutter?

Decluttering will get you out of a rut and give you more energy. I have seen this with my own eyes. My husband Ken transformed *overnight* after a huge decluttering session in the attic of his house. One day, he was a guy who was stagnant, super lazy, and unwilling to do anything; the next morning, he was all, "Oh my God, I wanna do more!". It was crazy.

Decluttering gives you a clearer head and greater confidence. You feel lighter and happier because old layers fall away. You have more respect for yourself because you're not holding onto the past and items that hold you back. You reconnect with your inner-self and your desires.

What are you making space for?

Why else would you declutter? Because you want to make space for your dreams. And calling in your dreams is potent. Give yourself the opportunity to think about those big dreams, because what you're holding onto is blocking the flow into your life. When you declutter and allow in all those dreams and desires, you'll want to be clear about just what that goodness is that you're welcoming in.

The magic of setting an intention

Many years ago, I was at a workshop with a wonderful lady who told me she wanted 'her own Ken' because she had heard all the stories of having this incredible partner in my life. Prompted by her declaration, I jumped into my PowerHouse Members Facebook group and ran a decluttering challenge. In the challenge, she set her intention for what she wanted and then she went and did all this decluttering. She was so dedicated. She was like a warrior doing all the clearing actions! Within a couple of weeks, she met an amazing new man. Guess what his name was? That's right, Ken!

When you let go of some of the clutter holding you back in your life, you'll welcome your dreams into your place.

EXERCISE: Set a decluttering intention

Before you start to declutter, there are some crucial steps you should be mindful of because the space you create can fill up with junk again quickly. This happened to another client of mine and she described it as 'decluttering hell'. She cleared out so much stuff, but her kids kept coming home from her ex-husband's with 'stupid plastic toys' and filling up the space again.

To stop that kind of thing from happening, you need to be 100% clear on what you're inviting into the space. Write down your intention for decluttering now. Declare what you're welcoming in.

CHAPTER 7

Physical and Emotional Clearing

When I moved to India, I got rid of thirty-four pairs of shoes and ten black bags of clothes. The only things I wasn't able to let go of were all my designer dresses. I'm talking about Vivienne Westwood, Moschino, and Christian Lacroix. Stunning pieces. I had bought these beautiful dresses over a series of eight years, perhaps one or two pieces each year for a wedding or special occasion. They were a huge financial investment, but also an emotional and energetic one because I wanted to have them in years to come. So I left for India and stored the dresses at my mum's house in her wardrobe.

Fast-forward four years. Those clothes were still hanging in my mum's wardrobe and she was doing a declutter of her own. She decided to declutter her wardrobe and found those dresses inside an inner cupboard. They had been there for that long. During one of our long-distance conversations, she asked me if I wanted them.

"Oh Patricia, what about those dresses?" And I thought she was talking about some old ballgowns that we'd had as kids, so I replied, "Oh yeah, you can get rid of those. I don't want them."

A couple of months later, I went back home for a visit and I happened to think about the designer dresses. I opened the inner cupboard of the wardrobe and they were all gone. I looked all around the house and asked my mum, "Where are the dresses?" And she told me she'd taken them to the charity shop. "You told me I could get rid of them."

What?!

Turns out she hadn't meant the old ballgowns. She'd been talking about those expensive, beautiful designer dresses.

It was a huge process for me to let them go. But they were gone. I was emotional about the loss of those dresses, so I went for a walk along the promenade up on the west coast of Galway, in Ireland. As I walked off the emotion, I realised all those dresses were attached to a different version of me. They were attached to the Patricia I was before I went to India, the Patricia who was totally into designer clothes, the Patricia who was materialistic. The old version of me, not the spiritual, beautiful, Feng Shui-loving me. I'd been deeply unhappy back then and put my worth on having these dresses, drinking, and driving fancy cars. There were loads of experiences with exes attached to those dresses too. So even though I cried, got angry, and felt a lot of emotions from the ties to those material possessions, it was all a necessary process of letting go.

A couple of months after I let go of those dresses and the associated emotional ties, after releasing all those stories and events about my exes, Ken and I got married. In letting go, I'd been really clear about what I wanted with this relationship.

Decluttering your home so that you welcome in your dreams can be both physical and emotional. Keep that in mind as you go into this exercise and be gentle with yourself. Remember decluttering is a constant process. You don't have to do it all today.

EXERCISE: Declutter your home

1. Download yourself a copy of my decluttering checklist www.patricialohan.com/happyhome bonuses from here or tick it off at the end of the chapter
2. Decide which area to focus on for your decluttering session and declutter intensely and completely.
3. Remembering your intentions, take each item in turn and ask yourself the following questions, paying particular attention to any memories or experiences associated with them. For example, if there is an ex-partner attached to an item it could be holding you back from new love, or

that old job's paperwork could be holding you back from the new career or role that you want.

Does it spark joy?

Do I really love it?

Does it fit?

Does it work or is it broken?

Is it depleting me?

Am I attached to it in some way?

Am I holding on to it, trying to hold on to some part of the past?

Am I keeping it because it was given to me by a certain person?

Is there a story behind keeping it?

4. Now, as you look and think about each item, decide what you will welcome instead. Turn to these questions now:

Where am I going?

What am I trying to create in my vision?

Decluttering tricks

If you're having trouble with decluttering, whether you're struggling to get started, or have got a bit stuck, here are some practical tricks to give you a kick-start.

Three-box method

Get yourself three boxes to put your stuff into and label them: 'keep', 'maybe', and 'get rid of'. Instead of a box, you could also make piles.

When you look at each item, if your thoughts are something like, "I'm definitely keeping that", it goes on the 'keep' pile. Then it's onto the next thing. If it's, "I'm definitely getting rid of that", easy! Onto the next one.

By the end, you'll have a nice variety. You'll know what you're getting rid of and what you're keeping and have a 'maybe' pile that you can come back to when you're ready to go through it again.

Embrace giving

Everything you get rid of goes to a charity shop, to recycling, or even for sale on eBay. There are so many good ways to let go of different items. You may even make some money or be able to gift some of your stuff to a better cause.

Come back later

Sometimes you may have to wait a while before you tackle the 'maybe' pile. Usually, I will leave those items in a box and write a note of what's in it. Then, if I haven't looked for those items within two weeks, I know I haven't been using them regularly. That's when I go back to the box and try to guess what's in it. If I can't remember, I must be hanging onto that stuff for some unknown reason. If I have no idea what that reason is, I get rid of it.

Partner up

You might choose to work with someone who is clear on saying 'yes' or 'no' to you on the items to keep or discard. Take the 'maybe' pile and hold up each item to your partner. *Yes, no, no, yes, no, yes, yes.* Just like that.

For me, that person is usually Ken. He'll say, "No, get rid of it. I hate it. I'm sick of looking at it. That has a rip in it. That doesn't look right anymore." Or he might go, "That's a great piece. I like it. That looks really good."

Do this for everything in your home.

Inch it out

There might be stuff in your home that you know you need to get rid of. You know deep in your heart something needs to go, but you're not quite ready to let it go.

Move those items you're still attached to a bit closer to the door. As items move closer to the door physically, you are energetically letting them go as well.

In a few months' time, when you want to clear more out, go back to those items first. You'll probably think, *why did I hold on to this?*

For example, perhaps you have been given a gift and you feel a bit guilty because you think it was expensive. Put it into a bag, take it closer to the door, and come back to it in a few months.

EXERCISE: Deep clean

Once you've done your physical clear-out and removed the layers of emotion that have been weighing you down and keeping energy blocked and stuck, a deep clean can feel oh-so good. Whether you do this job yourself or hire someone to clean for you, you'll find even more stuff to clear out and more layers of emotion to release.

1. After decluttering, do a deep clean. Get into all the nitty-gritty corners and clean deeply. It's not just the stuff you can see but the skirting boards, the walls, the pictures. Clean them all.

A friend in Bali did a deep clean of one of her bathrooms. In her love and marriage area, she found a dead bird. Now, this being Bali, animals get in, because the houses are so open. But even so, if something is dead in any area of the house, even insects or cobwebs; that is stagnant energy.

Giving the house a good clean means you're washing away all the memories and all the emotions. You're embodying it. You will see things you never even realised were there. And you'll be so grateful once you've cleared them all away.

EXERCISE: Fix what's broken

If something is broken it is depleting the energy of the area it is in. You'll learn all about those areas in Part Three, but for now, know that every area of your house represents a different area of your life and something broken in that area of your house means that area of your life will be 'broken' too.

Whether it's a broken ladder, a cracked vase, or a lamp that doesn't work, the place where you find it means that area won't be booming at that time.

So, get it fixed or let it go! Doing that will make the energy flow for something new and better to come in. Make sure everything in your home is flowing easily and happily

Decluttering Checklist

Declutter intensely and completely

Clothes	Done
Tops and bottoms	
Dresses	
Pajamas	
Jackets	
Handbags	
Belts	
Hats, Scarves, & Gloves	
Shoes & Boots	
Socks & Underwear	
Jewellery	
Costumes	
Athletic Clothes	
Papers	**Done**
Coupons & Receipts	
Tax Files	
Warranties & Manuals	
Important Documents	
Bills	
Greeting Cards	
Wrapping Paper	
Cheque Books	
Lecture Notes	
Business Cards	
Recipes	

Books	Done
Cookbooks	
General	
Kids	
Magazines	
Reference & Textbooks	
Phone Books	
Miscellaney	Done
General DVDs & CDs	
Video Games	
Cards & Remotes	
Craft Supplies	
Pet Supplies	
Coins	
Kids' Stuff	Done
Kids' Toys	
Bath Toys	
Outdoor Toys	
Sports Equipment	
Board Games	
Puzzles	
Cleaning Supplies	Done
Cleaning Sponges	
Scrubbers	
Rags	
Cleaning Products	
Mops	
Brooms	

Vacuums	
Buckets & Rubber Gloves	
Pest Control	
Laundry & Ironing Supplies	
Office	Done
Gift and Rewards Cards	
Office Supplies	
Appliances	
Computers	
Kitchen	Done
Fridges	
Coffee/Tea/Alcohol	
Supplements & Vitamins	
Utensils	
Silverware	
Knives	
Oven Mitts	
Pots & Pans	
Baking Sheets	
Baking Accessories	
Dishware	
Stemware	
Cups and Mugs	
Travel Cups & Water Bottles	
Paper Supplies	
Dishtowels & Aprons	
Misc	
Small Appliances Storage	

Décor	Done
Picture Frames	
Artwork & Mirrors	
Lamps	
Furniture	
Candles	
Pillows & Blankets	
Vases	
Tools & Hardware	Done
Maintenance Tools	
Gardening Supplies	
Light Bulbs	
Batteries & Flashlights	
Bathroom	Done
Medicine	
Skincare and Shaving	
Make-Up	
Brushes	
Hair Supplies & Brushes	
Samples & Travel Sizes	
Oral Hygiene Items	
Soap & Body Wash	
Perfume	
Feminine Supplies	
Linen	Done
Sheets	
Duvets	

Blankets	
Towels & Washcloths	
Sentimental Items	Done
Photos & Albums	
Journals & Diaries	
Memorable & Souvenirs	
Scrapbooks	
Personal Letters	
Heirlooms	
Trophies	

Be mindful. Decluttering is a never-ending process. It's like building muscle. The more you do, the easier it is to let go and release. If you are struggling with one particular thing, move on to a different section that is easier and less emotive.

Give yourself some space to do the decluttering, it's a journey (neverending). You can download the checklist from here:

www.patricialohan.com/happyhomebonuses

Sinead's Story

Sinead is a PowerHouse member based in Ireland. She is one of three sisters who are all part of our programme. She loves the PowerHouse community and especially loves that members of her family are involved with Feng Shui too. However, when Sinead joined the Feng Shui programme, her husband thought she was nuts. Little did he know, one of her goals was to manifest a new job for him.

> *"I joined the programme and my husband was like, 'Are you completely nuts? Feng Shui is a load of crap.'*
>
> *But in the career area of our home, I literally wrote job specs for him that he didn't even know about. I said things like 'He works in a great company. He has a company car. He has a bigger salary. He has sick pay. He has better holidays. He works with people who respect him.*
>
> *After about eight months, we got this phone call out of nowhere. He was offered an interview for a position that matched all the affirmations I wrote for him. And two weeks later, after two interviews, he got the job.*

This is amazing. Sinead's husband didn't even know about the affirmations she had written for him, and he still benefited just from living in a Feng Shui-ed home.

Then we asked her about her own job and what happened there.

"I was working three days a week as a school secretary, which was a job that I loved. I had good holidays, but I kept thinking about how it could be better. I wanted a few more hours. A week after I had been thinking about this, my friend told me about a job opportunity in a secondary school near me. I hadn't done a job interview in about ten years, and there were over 120 applicants.

And I got the job! They doubled my salary, and I only have to work one extra day a week. I have more holidays, and the school is only five minutes away from where I live."

We love to hear when our members get these unexpected wins. And notice how it wasn't right away for Sinead. She said that the phone call to her husband took about eight months. But she didn't lose faith. She kept doing the work and stayed true to her intentions.

"The amount of money that's come into my house in the last few years is just mind-boggling. My whole experience has been 100% positive from joining the PowerHouse community."

CHAPTER 8

Energetic Clearing and Sacred Space Clearing

Some things you want to let go of but you're not ready to yet, and that's okay. If you want to release those items quickly so that they are out of your energy field and you can welcome in brand new amazing dreams, you sometimes have to declutter and deal with the emotions first. Then you can remove the physical item from your home.

Doing a Sacred Space Clearing.

We have looked at all of the physical clutter in your home. Literally, every single square inch of your home has now been analysed, decluttered, and cleared, or hopefully, you now know what action you need to take next.

We're going to do an **energetic declutter** now, which is so powerful, so beautiful, and so profound, and is something that you can do whenever you feel something is a little off. In fact, this practice is one of my favourite things to do in a house when things have been feeling a little bit off.

It's called a **Sacred Space Clearing** — don't be put off by the word 'sacred'. Doing it the way that I'm going to teach you; you're going to love it, and you will start to feel a lightness as you move around the house, especially if you have already done the meditation to connect with the soul of your home because it will make such a difference.

What exactly *is* sacred space clearing then?

I am going to suggest several different tools that are part of ancient rituals that you can use to just clear an energetic layer of negative energy that could be hanging around your home. It's another form of decluttering, except what we are clearing is an invisible type of negative energy that stays in spaces until you do a space clearing. And we're going to get it out of your home. Yay!

The first thing, when you want to do a sacred space clearing, is to get yourself organised with the correct tools or the items that you want to use. There are no hard or fast rules about what to use or not to use. You can use a clearing tool of your choice or more than one.

There's no right or wrong way of doing this, but I'm giving you a sequence that has worked for me for years.

The first one is a clearing tool that uses sound.

For many years, as part of the work in my holistic therapy practice, I used Tibetan singing bowls, gongs, bells, and chimes. If you have any of these, you can use them. They are so powerful that the energy from them shifts the energy in a space easily.

How does it shift energy, you might be thinking? Well, imagine you are near a loud drum and you can feel the drumming sound vibrate in your body.

That's exactly why we use sound, because the sound will permeate into the cells of the house, and it will feel it and shake it. It gives a little rattle and a bit of a shake, and it cleanses the heavy and stagnant energy hanging around.

I have a beautiful sound-healing audio that I created using the singing bowls that is going to be downloadable for you to use. So if you don't have your own Tibetan bowl, you can just play the music to clear the space, along with the other steps I outline here.

You don't even need to go and buy an instrument if you don't have one, you could play the sounds and wander around into the corners and clap your hands or sing a song. The first time I ever did a space clearing, I used a saucepan and wooden spoon. As long as you are using something that makes a sound, it will work.

The second tool you can use is smudge sticks. White Sage is very popular, and this is not the sage that you grow or use for cooking. This is sacred White Sage that you can get at holistic stores or buy online. It's easy to come by now in health food shops too.

The other one I suggest is Palo Santo, from South America, which is a little wooden stick which you burn.

You can use incense, but it's not as effective. Although it's a lot about the intention, and intention plus action equals results.

I also love having some rose water to finish off. This isn't a necessity but it's a lovely addition to the process.

Once you have the tools you are going to use, you're ready to space clear!

If after you read this you think, "My family will think I'm bonkers," maybe wait until they've all gone out to do the space clearing.

Open all the windows, because when you start clearing the energy you want it to leave. You don't want to move it back around the house. If it's super cold where you are right now and there's snow outside, that's totally fine, you don't have to open all the windows. Even energetically and intentionally opening one window a small, little bit, will still work. As long as you have a place to send out the negative energy.

The third step is energetically protecting yourself, as you don't want to absorb any of that energy you are clearing into your energy field. I highly recommend you take one minute before you do anything (even if it sounds weird). Close your eyes and imagine a bubble of light around you.

Connect yourself with the earth and imagine your feet growing roots and sinking all the way down, down, down, down, down, down into Mother Earth, and then seeing a beam of light flowing down from the sky into the crown of your head so you're in a channel of light.

On the outside of that bubble of light, imagine that it's reflective, so it's almost mirrored. Anything that you are moving energetically out the windows and out of the house is not going to be absorbed into your energy field, because you are reflecting it away.

In this moment, drop into your heart, and connect with what your intention is for your home. Whatever it is you're calling in, whatever it is you're welcoming in, be really clear with that intention and drop into your heart and allow that to be the mantra or the intention as you move around your home.

Now, you can use any clearing tool of your choice. I usually start with sound and then use sage afterwards.

Start at your front door with the bowl, music, or sage, then move around your house clockwise, go into every little corner, behind the couches, into the places you haven't been in ages, into the cupboards you never open, into all the spaces with the sounds or sage, cleansing them all out.

As you move around you might see smoke coming from the sage or hear the bell sounding different, and this often happens with the singing bowls moving around the space. It sounds different, like it is absolutely amazing that bowl can sound so different.

If it feels heavy, or maybe the sound isn't as clear in some areas, make some extra sound in that area, clap your hands a little more, or sing a song that you love. Really just allow that sound to permeate through. You will feel a literal shift, and I bet you, if you tune into your house, and ask her what she feels afterwards, she would say, "Oh, relieved. I feel great."

Once you have finished, you can spritz some rose water to bring sweetness into the house and fill the space with the essence of rose.

Afterwards, I would recommend having a shower to wash away anything that came up and even spending some time outside in nature to ground yourself.

You can download the audio to use in the background for the Space Clearing of Tibetan Bowls I recorded for you here: www.patricialohan.com/happyhomebonuses

I've got so many different clients who have felt huge shifts after they've done this exercise. So, feel the connection, the intention, and just get those few items. Whether it's just incense, and you use your hands and clap or play the sound healing music, it all works.

I'm telling you now, this is powerful. I remember doing a space clearing in a business and, the next morning, new customers came in. The business had been open for three years and people came in that day and started asking the restaurant if it was new. Honestly, it was like a layer had been removed from the building and it was being seen for the first time by some people.

In Part Two, you've made huge physical shifts and your home may be looking vastly different from when you started reading this book. In all likelihood, it will be feeling different too. You may have noticed that Part Two has echoed Part One in its focus on clearing away the unwanted energy to make way for better energy. You have gone through your home on a much more granular level, considering every detail, and taking stock of every item.

To progress, you now need to map your home, see how every area corresponds to your life and use specific Feng Shui insights to optimise each one. Shifts may well be happening in your home already just from the powerful clearing you have undergone in Parts One and Two. Now it's time to get technical and tactical!

PART 3

Feng Shui for Your House

CHAPTER 9

Styles of Feng Shui

Flying Stars Classical Feng Shui, the style I practice and teach, is different from the Western version you may have heard of. A number of times, clients have come to me after doing Feng Shui and told me it hasn't worked. Since I know it *should* work, I've investigated what they have been doing. Usually, what has happened is they have Googled, "Feng Shui for bedrooms", and got confusing results. It's not necessarily that what they've researched is *wrong* as such. Often, it is right, but wrong when used in a certain form.

The confusion comes down to the difference in mapping, a technique that you're going to learn properly in the next chapter. Often, when you look up a Feng Shui plan online, Google will bring up a Feng Shui map for Western Feng Shui. The fact is Western Feng Shui was simplified and broken down in a generalised way for the West, making it much less effective. Western Feng Shui maps use the front door as the entry point. In Western Feng Shui, the entry point then dictates the locations of the different areas of your home. Flying Stars Classical Feng Shui, on the other hand, uses compass directions to determine the different areas. It is much more accurate. You can see then how Feng Shui advice can easily be applied wrongly following Western Feng Shui, even when the advice itself is not necessarily wrong.

As we established earlier, Feng Shui is all about intentional focus. In ancient times, houses were built to align with the most auspicious directions for each life area. As such, each home had its own unique energetic blueprint. In *The Happy Home*, you are learning, as far as possible, the basic principles of Flying Stars Classical Feng Shui, as it applies to your home. I say "as far as possible" because your home, of course, has its own personality and energetic blueprint, which we create a personalised home report for in our signature PowerHouse Programme.

You've already dug into some of the initial layers of Feng Shui by clearing the past and decluttering your home. The next step is to map the different areas of your home so that your decluttering can become more specific and intentional, and even more potent for you to manifest your desires and have a supportive home. This will mean identifying nine areas of your home and how they correspond to the different aspects of your life. The practice from there will be curating the specific, underlying, hidden energies happening in your home and curing any problems with those.

Maria's Story

Maria is an Empowerment Coach and works with clients who are open-minded and are willing to reconnect with a deeper part of themselves.

She was one of the first to join my signature PowerHouse Programme when she was looking for ways to feel more supported and to improve her health after having a baby.

After becoming a life coach in 2007, she decided to learn other techniques that would help her to explore deeper within the self. She became a Journey practitioner, Quantum Healing practitioner, and a healer and channel, to name just a few. Creating her own technique, called 'Source Energy Healing', which she has been using with clients since 2010, she has found it very effective for transformative healing.

Maria believes people should nurture and clean their energy on a daily basis, and that's part of her teaching.

> *"I have always been a very hands-on type of person. It's great to know something, but it's another level to use it, to apply it to your life, and that's my philosophy, and why I started teaching people. I want people to have tools and techniques which will help them transform their lives and to feel great about themselves."*

Where does Feng Shui fit into this?

> *"I've been using Black Hat Feng Shui for decades and never realised there are different schools of Feng Shui until I met Patricia. Since I've done the programme with Patricia, I have learned a completely new outlook on Feng Shui. I decided to invest in PowerHouse and get a personalised home report. When I placed all the remedies in my house, the differences I found there were just unbelievable. I felt so supported and loved by my house. And I've never felt like that before. It's just wonderful, and the changes my family experienced are amazing! I fully got back to my health which was my main goal. My relationship with my husband has blossomed. Wonderful opportunities started to appear and we had a year of getting everything at half price!*
>
> *I personally treat Feng Shui as part of my own support structure and when I feel supported, I can support others in a better way."*

CHAPTER 10

Mapping Your Home

Having cleared up any misconceptions about what we're doing here, let the detailed planning commence! You will now learn how to draw a map of your home and find the unique energy spots that in Feng Shui we call Power Centres. In traditional Chinese Feng Shui, they are called *Guas*, but in PowerHouse, we translate them as Power Centres of your home. These energy spots are the basis of everything else you're going to learn about Feng Shui, so your floor plan will become your treasure map for this work.

Creating floor plans

To do the important job of marking up your floor plan and finding out where in your home your nine Power Centres or living areas are, your first task is to grab a copy of the plans of your home. If you built your house yourself, you probably have these plans. When you bought your home, your realtor might have given you the plans. Sometimes when you rent a place, your property manager or letting agent has the plans available for you. It's important that you can write on the plans, so once you've found them, make a copy. And if you've made any adjustments such as an extension, remember to add that in. If you have accurate architectural plans already, you're one of the lucky ones, as that makes this job so easy.

What if you don't have the plans for your home? No problem! You can create a floor plan easily with a great free tool called floorplanner.com. All you'll need to do is measure your home. Once you have the measurements, enter them all into the tool. It's vital that your plans are to scale and the correct shape. However, you only need the shape and size of your house or apartment, not the fixtures, fittings, furniture, or windows. Don't worry about the garden either, as it's just the outline of the house we are working with in this book.

If you prefer to draw your floor plan by hand, you can use a sheet of graph paper, a pencil, and a ruler. You'll also need a measuring tape, but even if a measuring tape isn't available, you can still draw a proportional plan of your home. I've been known to count out the proportions of homes with my feet! All you have to do is put one foot in front of the other and count. For ease, I use one square of graph paper per foot, keeping it simple.

No matter which tool you use, it is crucial to make sure the **outline of your home** is accurate, meaning the length and breadth of your house, and any extra irregular parts that stick in or out. If you wish, you may also mark the bedroom, bathroom, and kitchen areas in, to get an idea. Even though Feng Shui ignores the interior walls of your house, you may want to mark them as a guide, for your own information.

What happens if you live in a house that has more than one storey? If you live in a two-storey house where the upstairs has exactly the same outline as the downstairs, you will not need to do a second-level floor plan for the upstairs, because you can easily find your Power Centres for both storeys, based on one plan. If any additional storeys are not the same shape as the ground floor, you will need to draw another floor plan for each one.

What are the Power Centres of your home?

Once you have completed your floor plan, you'll need to divide it into nine areas by dividing the length into three equal parts and the breadth into three equal parts as well, like a grid. In other words, measure the length and divide it by three, then measure the width and divide it by three. Draw in the lines across your home. It's important to note that you are looking at the main length and width of the home, ignoring any protruding parts or alcoves. You'll deal with those separately.

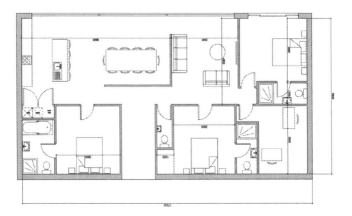

Floorplan of a Straight Forward House

What happens if your house is an uneven shape? This happens all the time! For Feng Shui, the dream shape of a house would be a rectangle. It's great to know this for buying or building houses in the future because that makes it easy to Feng Shui. However, it may be the case that you are in an odd-shaped house with bits sticking in or out. This is likely to mean that you will be missing one, or several, Power Centres. When there is a missing Power Centre in a home, the capacity for that home to expand into its fullest potential in that area is lost. This can have huge ramifications for the lives of the residents in that home.

Here's how we tackle non-rectangular shapes. First, you need to determine whether the piece of the house that doesn't fit the rectangle shape is an 'extra bit' or a 'missing bit'. If the length and/or width of the shape or protrusion is less than 50% of the length or width of the floor plan, you can take it to be an extension or an 'extra bit'. This means it becomes part of the Power Centre it is attached to already. However, if the length and/or width of the protrusion is more than 50% of the length or width of the floor plan, it is part of the house shape. That means you have a missing Power Centre, a partially missing Power Centre or several missing Power Centres.

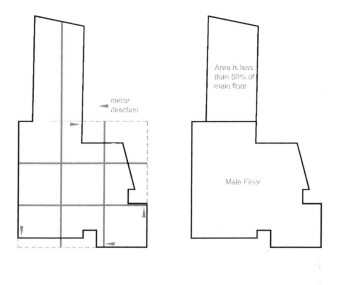

Diagram with Extention & Missing Guas

Once you have determined where you may have a missing Power Centre, extend the line of your home to create a rectangle. Use a dotted line to signify that it is a missing bit.

Mark the Power Centres on your floor plan for every level of the house. Each storey might be missing different Power Centres depending on the shape of the house and whether the floors are copies of one another or completely dissimilar.

Ultimately, your floor plan should look like a rectangle, perhaps with extra or missing bits, and with nine equal-sized areas: three Power Centres on the length by three Power Centres on the width; or eight outer Power Centres and a central one.

Compass reading

Now that you have a floor plan marked with a grid of the nine Power Centres, you'll need to know which Power Centre corresponds to which area of the floor plan and, therefore, your house. This is where the compass directions come in! As I touched on before, Flying Stars Classical Feng Shui relies on the directions of the compass to orientate the Power Centres.

Taking a compass reading is not a complicated task but take care to ensure you get it right. You can use a regular camping compass or the built-in compass on your smartphone. If you don't have a compass, download a free app to your Android or iPhone.

INSTRUCTIONS

1. Remove jewellery and coins from your person. Stand right *outside* your house with your back to the front door. Make sure you don't go near any cars, step out three or four feet from the house. Stand with your compass in front of you and level. Make sure you are using magnetic north. (This is the normal setting for a smartphone compass and regular camping compass).

2. Look at the compass and see what direction it points to. Mark this on your floor plan, just behind you. If you are facing north, you can fill in the opposite direction as south on your plan. The same goes for the other directions. If you are facing east, fill in the west direction on the plan.

3. Repeat the reading three times in different places, for example, by walking a few paces to one side of the front door, and then a few further paces to the other side of the door. This is super important! If you only do one reading and it's really far off, that will throw the whole exercise off. If you do three readings and get one anomaly, you will be able to see that easily. It could be because something is interfering with the compass.

Don't worry if it's not perfect!

Marking out your floor plan and getting it exact is not imperative. As I've said this book is a beginners guide to get you started, so you don't have to have this floor plan down to an exact science! Just do your best. Realising and having the awareness that you have nine different areas of your home — and that each one represents a different part of your life — will definitely improve the energy alone!

The recommendations that we have in this book are just intentional remedies. They are not the precise remedies that we would do in PowerHouse. Now, if a client did come to us in PowerHouse, we would take all their information and map out a very precise floorplan and give the exact remedies that need to go into each area. That would have a super specific, dramatic affect on the energy in that area!

But what were doing is just merely intentional. You're not doomed if you put a mirror in the wrong place. For this book — don't sweat it. Don't overthink it. Just do this floorplan as a rough guide and get an idea of where the areas are. And then write the intentions and follow the steps. Even if you just get the basic nine areas and directions sorted, you're already beginning to Feng Shui.

It's the intention and awareness that's the most important part in this — not getting it perfect.

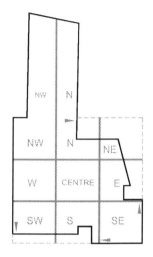

**Diagram of House with all the
Directions Marked on the Plan**

Filling in missing Power Centres
with mirrors and crystals

As I've mentioned, having a missing area can have
serious negative impacts on your life, so you want to
deal with those missing Power Centres in order to reach
your full potential.

A client of mine who had done Western Feng Shui
for many years had a missing Power Centre in her
home. She thought it was her prosperity area, which
didn't make much sense in her life. When we started
working together with Flying Stars Classical Feng Shui,

she discovered her missing Power Centre was actually her family and community area. When she had this revelation, everything started making sense. She had bought the house five years earlier and immediately had a falling out with her family, who lived overseas. She told me, "When I bought this house, my whole family basically disappeared." Notice that word ... *disappeared?* The capacity of her home in the area of family and community was simply not available.

What is the solution, then, when you have a missing area?

You will need to **build new walls energetically** to create the space for that Power Centre. In other words, you're going to fake it! Wherever on your floor plan you have dotted lines, you are going to pretend those walls are there. Don't worry. I'm not going to ask you to build any makeshift structures! All you are going to do is use mirrors to create the space.

EXERCISE: Creating walls

1. Gather some compact mirrors or buy some mirror tiles from a dollar shop. The sizes and shapes of the mirrors you use don't matter.
2. Take your floor plan and look at where you have dotted lines. From inside the house, place the shiny reflective side of a mirror facing the nearest wall to your missing Power Centre, projecting outwards towards where you want your wall to be.

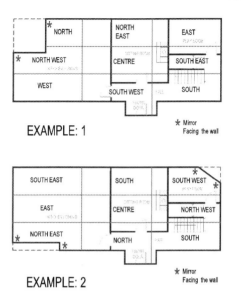

EXAMPLE: 1

✱ Mirror
Facing the wall

EXAMPLE: 2

✱ Mirror
Facing the wall

House Example of Missing Guas – where to locate mirrors

3. The mirror can even be hidden and can be anywhere along the wall, even right at the top of it, or in a corner out of the way. If you don't want it to look too obvious, you can paint the back of the mirror or hide it behind a piece of furniture.

4. Next, you'll need some small pointy clear quartz crystals. When you're filling in the Power Centre, just pop two or three of those crystals into the ground. If you can't put the crystals in, just focus on the mirrors. Alternatively, you could use lights in the corner of the borderline of the wall; anything to draw that energy in.

If you have missing areas in the place where you're living, it can be having a serious impact on your life. And this mirror exercise may not seem all that important but let me demonstrate the impact it can have. Remember my client whose family 'disappeared' from her life? She added a mirror facing the walls of her home to create energetic walls. She got shivers in her whole body as she placed them there. Later that day, out of nowhere, and after five years of no contact, her father rang her. She had given her house the capacity to hold that family and community space.

CHAPTER 11

Overview of the Nine Areas of Your Home

Here's where we dive into the nitty-gritty. By now, you have your floor plan, your Power Centre grid, and your compass directions. You have identified any missing Power Centres and energetically filled in those areas with mirrors and crystals. Once you've marked up the plan of your home, the tricky technical part is done. Now we're going to look at the nine different areas of your home, the way they function, and how they affect your day-to-day life.

As you now know, each of the nine areas on the grid you've drawn onto your floor plan corresponds with, and affects, the outcomes in specific areas of your life. So, what are these areas, and what do they mean and represent? And, most importantly, how do they affect your life?

You need to consider what you can add to improve the area, think about what is going on in that aspect of your life and home, and see what conclusions you can draw from the state of that area.

Power Centres of your home

Here's an overview of the nine areas of your home and what aspect of your life they govern.

Central:	Health and well-being
North:	Career and life journey
Northeast:	Wisdom and knowledge
East:	Family and community
Southeast:	Prosperity and abundance
South:	Fame and reputation
Southwest:	Love and relationships
West:	New beginnings, creativity, and fertility
Northwest:	Helpful people and travel

Before moving on and looking at each of these in more detail, take some time to notice what comes up when you learn what each area represents. In your journal, write down any instant reactions or insights that you have upon learning what these Power Centres are.

Enhancements

In the following nine chapters, I will give recommendations for enhancing each area of your life by adding in certain items that represent a happy, healthy, wealthy state, or removing any items that may be causing negativity in that area.

Of course, your ability to implement these recommendations may depend on whether anyone else who lives in your home (your partner and/or family) is on board with this Feng Shui process or not. I encourage you to do everything you can to get them on board because it is so powerful when you are free to enhance areas in line with what I suggest.

You are about to delve into each Power Centre more specifically now. Every time you work with a new Power Centre, it's important to do the inner work to become clear on your intentions for that area.

Deities

One layer of Feng Shui incorporates spiritual deities. Some of my recommendations may include adding statues of such gods or goddesses to an area.

This doesn't mean you need to add a physical statue necessarily; it's more about tuning in to specific energy through a representation. More importantly, I would never recommend that you add anything that doesn't feel right. The energy has to resonate with you.

As you move through the next nine chapters, I will suggest different deities. For example, adding a small Ganesh, the elephant-faced Hindu god, known as the remover of obstacles. If Ganesh feels like the right deity for you, print off a small picture and keep it in that area of your home. If not, you don't have to use any representation of that deity. It's not obligatory.

If it feels better to you, you may replace one suggested deity with another. For example, if I make the suggestion to add Lakshmi, the goddess of prosperity, you may substitute her for the goddess Fortuna. I suggest looking up the gods and goddesses to decide if they are right for you or if you would like to find an alternative.

If you really love the sound of a particular deity, you might get a small figurine for the area of your home requiring extra support. What is important to keep in mind is that the decision lies with you. It is **your house**. You do not need to fill it with anything that doesn't feel right for your life or the people in your home.

Affirmations

I also invite you to write affirmations and place them in specific areas of the home. Affirmations are like a letter written directly to the universe, opening you up to fully receive. They are also a wonderful opportunity for you to become clear on what you want. You are the one planting the seeds in your life. Affirmations can be anywhere from two lines to two pages — it depends on how much you feel like writing. They can be expanded upon and evolve at any time.

Your affirmations are private and so shouldn't be shared with everyone that enters your home. Give the seeds a chance to root deeply before revealing too much.

As before with the deity advice, affirmations don't need to be massive and plastered up on the wall like a huge poster. You may like to write down an affirmation for every area and place each one in an envelope to keep in a corresponding part of your home. You are welcome to hide them in a picture frame or drawer/cupboard. Nobody needs to see them or know they are there.

As ever, it's all about intention. Simply spend some time affirming your intentions. Just make sure, when you write affirmations, that you keep the language in the present tense. Always write that you are grateful for it happening, then act as if it already has.

Here is a sample affirmation:

"I am grateful that I have balance and harmony in all areas of my life, including perfect mental, physical, and spiritual health. Thank you."

You may also write your overall intention or vision for your home. Put this into an envelope and pop it into an area that feels good.

Continue journaling as you make enhancements to each area and see the energy change. Journaling will give you the juice for creating your affirmations because you will be able to see your intentions clearly and should also write about what you have learned in each area. Note that the affirmations given in the following chapters are sample affirmations only. I encourage you to write your own. In fact, the more specific you are with your affirmations — what the intention is, how you want to spend your time, who you want to be involved with, how you intend for it to happen — the more easily it will unfold. Your house hears you. It supports you all the way.

Lastly, when it comes to calling in your intentions, pace yourself. Take your time. You have a lot of information coming up about the nine Power Centres and how to enhance each one, but all of these enhancements don't need to be done today or tomorrow. Spend time intentionally going through every single area, and it will make an epic difference in your home and your life.

CHAPTER 12

The Health and Well-Being Area

The first Power Centre is smack bang in the centre of your home and represents health, well-being, unity, self-love, self-acceptance, and gratitude. The state of this area of your home will affect your vibrancy, your energy, and your sense of looking after yourself. This area has a powerful effect on your life overall and underpins everything.

Many years ago, I was working with a client. As she took me around her home so that I could get familiar with it, she came to the central Power Centre and introduced it by saying, "Welcome to the dumping ground." This accurately represented the state of her family's health and it was no wonder. As part of our work together, we cleared out that central area. After decluttering an enormous amount of stuff from that space, her father, who had been sick and unable to play golf for two years, went out and played eighteen holes!

Enhancements

- Make sure the central area is clear of clutter
- Add a bowl of fresh fruit or a vase of flowers
- Keep this area nice and organised
- Ensure there is nothing broken here
- Keep self-care and healthy recipe books in this area
- Call in the energy of compassion and love to the centre area of your life
- Add a statue of the goddess Quan Yin, known as the goddess of mercy and compassion.

Affirmations

"I am grateful that everyone is getting along with each other."

"I am grateful that I am vibrant, happy, and healthy."

"I am grateful I am perfectly healthy in body, mind, and spirit."

Joanna's Story

Joanna is a PowerHouse member who lives in Northern New South Wales in Australia. She helps people achieve financial freedom through small, easy investments.

Joanna began her Feng Shui journey after moving into what she thought was her dream home. It seemed to have everything going for it; it was beautiful, expansive, near the beach, and even had its own swimming pool! But as soon as she moved in, two of her major clients ceased their work with her. She is a naturally optimistic person, but this was just too much.

She also noticed that her relationships became tense and frustrated. It just seemed that everything started to go wrong after she moved into her new home.

After discovering the PowerHouse programme, she decided that she could make her "dream home" an actual Dream Home. She just had to do some work with it and change the energy.

We asked Joanna what happened once she got her home report and started to implement her Feng Shui remedies.

> *"Out of the blue, I had a tax refund come through. And very quickly other big chunks of money started to come in. I also noticed that the worst part of my home, the area that needed a lot of work, was my community and friendship area. Patricia gave me all the remedies to sort this centre. After I did that, I'm happy to report that I have lots of friends again.*

I took the time to watch all the videos and do all the work in the programme. I went on little missions to get all the pieces I needed and get all my remedies in place. And I had to let go of some of the things I knew had been holding me back."

CHAPTER 13

The Career and Life Journey Area

The north Power Centre of your home represents your career and life journey, which includes your current job or the business you run, as well as what you want to do in the future. What is crucial to know here is that nothing is set in stone. You have to allow flexibility so that you can become whatever you may wish for in the future as your life unfolds. Your life's journey encompasses all different parts of your life, not necessarily just your job, but also the roles you play.

Consider all the roles you play in your life. Perhaps you are a daughter, a sister, a wife, or a mother. What do you want to do well in your journey? You may be a caregiver, a runner, a cyclist, a swimmer, or a stamp collector. What hobbies and interests do you have that you want to develop? Perhaps you wish to be a traveller, a speaker, or a community leader. These are all part of that journey.

Enhancements

When Steven Spielberg was going for his third Oscar, he engaged a Feng Shui consultant. She went to his house and one of the enhancements she made was to move his first two Oscar statues from his office into his career Power Centre. She then added a third (replica!) Oscar along with the two real ones to anchor the intention. He now has three real Academy Awards.

- Add items that represent you and your partner's career aspirations
- When going for a new job or promotion, place the job description and something symbolising the company in this area
- Place symbols of your desired career here
- Dream big about how you want your life to look
- Put up a list of your top interests
- Do the Create Your Dream Day exercise* and pin it on a wall in this area
- Include a spiritual statue of the goddess Quan Yin and/or Tara

When thinking about the roles you want to play and the activities you want to participate in, have some fun and think outside the box! Start dreaming about what you want deep in your heart. Forget about the 'how' and write down what you've always hoped to achieve in your career or life.

Affirmations

When I was training to be a yoga teacher and living in India, I didn't have a career per se. I used the first of these affirmations to move from being a trainee to getting paid well in a career. I didn't add the part about getting paid well for ages, yet I can look back and see how I was sowing the seeds for the life I later had. I didn't know at the time what I wanted to do, but I was certain I wanted to be around people I loved and who loved me. I wanted to express my creative talents. I wanted to enjoy what I did, and I wanted to be paid well.

Earlier I suggested being incredibly specific when writing affirmations, but it's understandable that you may not yet be clear on what you want. If you don't have a clear path, it is specific enough to affirm the experience and feelings you want every day. If you want to call in more clarity, try the second of these affirmations.

"I work at a job I truly enjoy, working with people I love and who love me, expressing my creative talents daily and getting well paid for it."

"I now have clarity and excitement about my fulfilling career path."

"I'm passionate about helping others live the life they deserve while earning abundantly."

"I use my unique skills and gifts to work in my perfect career, be of service, and live in joy and abundance."

"I have excellent relationships with everyone who works with me and for me."

"I attract the right clients, students, and employees for an abundant, fulfilling, rewarding, and successful career."

EXERCISE: Create your dream day

Get your journal out and using the guiding questions below, imagine your dream day. Write down a description of this dream day.

> *What are you doing on your dream day?*

> *How are you spending your time?*

> *Who are you with?*

> *Where are you?*

Dream big and think about if you had all the time, money, and opportunities in the world — how would you spend your day?

If you want to dive deeper into this exercise you can download a copy of my Dream Day Worksheet from here: www.patricialohan.com/happyhomebonuses

Stacey's Story

Stacey is an Occupational Therapist & Artist.

Before doing the PowerHouse programme, Stacey hadn't given herself a clear direction for her goals. She had kids and a business but wasn't spending enough time on self-care or living her life to its full potential, and she was aware of this.

> *"Before I tried PowerHouse, I had tried everything. I had been to healers, psychics, and business groups. I used to run away to the US every single year to recharge, and everything had its place, I guess. But I still had this nagging feeling, in my bones, that something was not quite right.*
>
> *I wasn't really sure what to expect. A group of my business friends and I decided to jump in together, so we would share the ride and the experience. The reason why I personally picked Patricia, is because I sat next to her at a conference and then I realised she was a speaker there. We had already chatted quite a lot. She was warm, friendly, energetic, and most importantly, she was real. Very authentic."*

The Powerhouse Signature Programme helped her to clear the clutter out of her mind, her life, and her house. She found clarity in her goals and put her faith in the process, setting clear intentions that she was going to buy her home and increase her income. And it worked. Within the timeframe she had set, she'd found her house and been offered work unexpectedly. She also started to paint, and people started asking if she was going to have an exhibition and whether they could purchase her work.

"Which is amazing, because I had never painted. It was just something that I knew was inside me, and that I wanted to do for self-care. I've also become really clear on my business, my life as a mum, and my self-care routines. It no longer feels like a circus. It feels really, really calm. Much calmer than it was before.

When all these results started happening, it made me realise the power of Feng Shui and setting clear intentions. I got exactly what I asked for. The house I bought ticked all of the boxes on my list, and the income figure that I intended on increasing monthly, was the exact figure that people offered me in the contracts.

Since engaging Patricia, I have stepped up into a knowledge that was always there inside me, but that I feel I didn't really fully believe until I saw it for myself. Anything is actually possible.

And who would she recommend the programme to?

"Women, business owners, mums, people who just feel stuck in their life and don't know why they cannot move forward. People who have runs of bad luck in their life. Feng Shui shows you why that is and it is quite astounding to understand why that might be happening!"

C H A P T E R   1 4

The Wisdom and Knowledge Area

The northeast Power Centre represents knowledge, self-cultivation, wisdom, intuition, and meditation. This is your spiritual and educational area, encompassing personal development and growth.

For the wisdom and knowledge area, you will need to become clear on what you want to learn, how you want to grow, and what spiritual growth you wish to experience. Ask yourself how you want to grow as a person and evolve. What ancient wisdom do you want to connect with? How do you want to activate your intuition?

Given its connections with the spiritual journey and meditation, this is the best place for an altar, where you can place objects representing self-cultivation anywhere within the area, hidden discreetly in a cupboard, hanging on a wall, or even behind a picture frame. It's not just a matter of shoving the encyclopaedias in that corner. This is intentional, remember. Get specific on what you wish to develop.

Enhancements

- If there is something you particularly want to learn, place a symbol of it in this area. If you want to learn to play the guitar, perhaps place an image of a guitar or a music book here
- Create a vision board with images that represent your dreams and desires. Have a look on Google or Pinterest if you want to find images or inspiration, and put it here
- Keep inspiring or educational books in this Power Centre
- Collect and display images of people who inspire you
- Place an owl figure in this location to symbolise wisdom and knowledge
- Create an altar or meditation area
- If you can't meditate here, because the layout of your home makes it impractical, keep spiritual statues, oracle cards, or some crystals here
- Connect this space and your meditation space energetically by placing something that represents your spiritual practice in the area — perhaps your meditation cushion

- If you're considering a career change or would like to acquire knowledge in a new area, keep related books, study materials, and degree prospectuses here
- Make this room a library or add a bookshelf

Affirmations

"I am grateful that I am learning constantly and that it's easy and enjoyable."

"I see myself growing continually in self-awareness and expanding my consciousness."

"I have an abundance of time and the ability to learn."

"I can expand in all the ways I choose."

"I am intuitive. I am connected to my own inner vision."

"I listen to my intuitive self. I trust and follow my intuition."

"I live in the now."

"I am connected to my true path and purpose. I see possibilities and bring them into my reality."

Laura's Story

Laura is a healer, a spiritual and Law of Attraction teacher.

One of her major focuses is on helping women who are struggling to fall pregnant to understand why they have chosen to include the energetic imprint that creates these issues within their soul contract in this lifetime and to help them release this so that they can create the family of their dreams.

> *"I recommend Feng Shui to everybody!! Feng Shui will change your life completely. It will shift your life perfectly in the right direction. It's one of the most effective programmes I've ever done. The best thing about your approach is how tailored to your own home it is. It's not generic in any way, it's very specific, and I love that about your programme. It's really powerful and I highly recommend doing it."*

Twenty-something years ago, while working in the corporate world, Laura underwent a personal tragedy, having a miscarriage. This experience was extremely spiritually transforming for her and changed her focus in life. Within a year of her loss, she was training to be an acupuncturist and starting to heal people.

She undertook every healing course she could and was a master in many of the healing modalities within two years. Clients started coming to her wanting to fall pregnant and her healing worked for them. She started mentoring the women in the Law of Attraction, and they started getting pregnant.

With the success she was having with mentoring wanna-be-mamas, Laura turned to how she could help women with other problems in the same way.

> *"Suddenly they started to turn up, asking me to help them with all sort of other issues, from problems with family members, exes and attracting narcissist relationships, to debt and money issues. As my practice is always full, other practitioners kept asking me questions about how I achieved this, so I started to mentor other practitioners on how to attract clients and they now have full practices too.*

So, where did the PowerHouse Feng Shui Programme fit into Laura's life?

> *"It was completely transformational for me. My office is in my house and the basics of just shifting my office around were unbelievable. It became a completely different environment and it felt completely different in there.*

Before I felt overwhelmed and couldn't concentrate. Now I am so productive, find it easy to concentrate and no longer feel overwhelmed, which has resulted in me helping more people and making more money than I have ever done before. It's been fantastic.

But more than that, it's a perception thing. You talked about having your home as your springboard, that when you're trying to move forward in certain ways the energy of your home keeps bringing you back to its vibration. As a healer, I know everything is energy, but it didn't click that, of course, your home is energy too, and having a vibrationally supportive base was actually a game-changer for me.

Feng Shui has shifted my vibrations and my abilities so much higher, and my perception and my connection with my guardian angels and all my team have shifted completely.

It's been really, really incredibly powerful. Amazingly powerful and I just love it! I recommend that everybody does Feng Shui now.

I've dabbled with Feng Shui for years but I hadn't really done it properly. I know about the Five Elements, of course as an acupuncturist, and I had wanted to employ a Feng Shui Consultant for a long time, so I tried to muddle through on my own. I should have known better. As I know from being an acupuncturist there are always ten ways to skin a cat in Chinese modalities, so of course, Feng Shui was going to be the same.

And what does she think it's good for?

"Everything, but especially if you're feeling stuck and you feel like you're going one step forward and two back. Feng Shui is the place to start.

I now believe that you attracted your home as the perfect match to your energy when you bought it. If you want to make changes in your home you need to raise the energy of it through Feng Shui, so that you can attract higher vibration people, money, situations and high vibe babies into your life.

Once your home is constantly vibrating on a higher frequency thanks to the Feng Shui placements, any internal energetic work such as releasing

energetic imprints, low vibe thoughts, feelings and beliefs will become so much easier for you to do and the Law of Attraction will result in creating a life of your dreams and NOT the opposite."

CHAPTER 15

The Family and Community Area

The east area of your home represents family and community. This relates to your own family, your extended family, and your in-laws. It also extends out to your community, such as the organisations you belong to, charities you support, and any clubs, sports, or online communities where you are a member. In essence, it is about the people with whom you surround yourself.

Enhancements

- Place photos of your family and friends in this area
- Print or collect images of your family crest or family tree
- Keep family photo albums here

- Add a picture or symbol of a group of people holding hands, or of a group you belong to yourself
- Have some fun making a beautiful collage of family photos with family mottos or mantras
- Energise the area with happy memories
- Include a spiritual statue of Hera, the goddess of family

Note: Don't put family photos in the bedroom, even if the bedroom corresponds with your family and community area. Your bedroom is to be used for totally different energy from this.

Affirmations

"I am blessed with a beautiful well-balanced family."

"I nurture and am nurtured by a wonderful family and friends, with love and kindness, patience and goodwill."

"I have an extended family filled with health, respect, and love."

"My family is healthy, happy, safe, and full of love."

"I am a source of love and inspiration for my family and friends, as they are for me."

"My family and friends are a beautiful reflection of divine love."

Anne-Marie's Story

Anne-Marie is a decluttering expert who was living in a house that was bad for both money and people.

She was in the financial sector for over eleven years but couldn't get her banking exams. She'd been decluttering from a young age because her father had been diagnosed with bone cancer and her mother took on the family farm where Anne-Marie started organising and putting structures in place. It took her a while to realise that was Feng Shui though.

She got into Feng Shui after the birth of her second child, although she didn't know at the time what the word 'decluttering' meant. She was living in a house that was at least a hundred and fifty years old and which must have contained a crazy amount of stories. She did a twelve-month decluttering course to move things on and to set up her own business:

> *"My business was set up in early March 2017 and has grown from strength to strength, with a waiting list of two or three months, and I've been able to take on an assistant! I suppose I put out to the universe what I wanted, what I was available for, and what I wasn't available for, and then the phone started ringing."*

And this was after joining my PowerHouse programme. What was the problem before joining the programme?

> *"Money was coming in, but it was flushing out just as fast. It'd barely even hit the bank account, and it was gone. We were struggling, to be quite honest. You know, I was down to the last pennies in the bank account, and just saying, "Where's the next money coming from?"*

And she saw that decluttering was the biggest part of the Feng Shui jigsaw, as it was about just letting go of the clutter in your life or home, where the stagnant energy was, and moving the blocks out the way so the magic could happen!

> *"When I started, there was a flow of money into our farm. My relationship with my husband ... totally changed. Intimacy blossomed, and we had better communication with each other. Everything changed. Fighting with bickering children is also nearly gone.*
>
> *If I hadn't gone through PowerHouse with you, I'd still be back there, probably crying into my pillow, which I'd been doing, because we were in dire straits. Instead, money is flowing, and clients are flowing ..."*

Feng Shui rocks, I'll tell you that! That was my keynote last year, and I'm still going with it, and it is life-changing. Whatever 'it' is. If you're having issues with your family, your money, your career, or just the general well-being of your house and everyone in it. Just do it!"

CHAPTER 16

The Prosperity and Abundance Area

In the southeast Power Centre of your home, the space represents wealth, prosperity, and abundance. This is not just about money, although it does include money. The wealth you see represented here includes the abundance of love, joy, happiness, connection, and friendships. An abundance of everything.

Enhancements

- Write a cheque to yourself from the universe for a large amount of money. You can download a version from www.patricialohan.com/happyhomebonuses and fill it out easily — or make one yourself
- Add a spiritual statue or representation of Lakshmi, the goddess of prosperity, or of Fortuna, the goddess of fortune

- Create a prosperity bowl of overflowing abundance. Get a small bowl and a small mirror. Put the mirror flat on a table. Place the bowl on the reflective side of the mirror and fill the bowl full of coins. It doesn't matter the type of coins, but ensure the bowl is overflowing. Every time you look at the bowl, affirm to yourself: "I have an infinite supply of money. I am abundant". The mirror symbolises a doubling of prosperity
- Add in luxury items that make you feel prosperous
- Add upward-growing plants such as bamboo, jade plants, or ferns
- Place images of items that make you feel abundant or prosperous
- Hang a picture of anything you consider abundant or that grows abundantly, such as a field of poppies or a forest of bluebells
- Include symbols or pictures of anything that represents wealth and abundance to you and your culture

Note: Any plant that is upward-growing is positive apart from cacti, which I don't recommend you have in the home. Bamboo is considered lucky. Jade plants are otherwise known as money plants or money trees. They are easy to grow and are prolific, which is why we relate them to prosperity. Both of these plants are considered great for increasing wealth.

Don't panic if you discover your prosperity area happens to be your bathroom or toilet. All you need to do is make it feel as luxurious as possible. If there is anything that does not feel abundant or beautiful in that area, declutter it, and make space to bring in new luxury or abundance. You might place a significant item or symbol of what you want to call in, or simply something that feels good, such as fresh towels, or a bowl filled and overflowing with coins.

Affirmations

"I'm willing to receive money for my pleasure."

"I'm willing to allow my life to be fun and easy."

"I'm a trust-fund baby of the universe."

"I'm a magnet to money."

"I deserve to be prosperous and wealthy. Money flows easily to me."

"Money and prosperity help me to help others. The more I give, the more I receive."

"I enjoy being paid for doing what I love."

Miriam's Story

Miriam is a manifesting mentor, who works with entrepreneurial women, teaching them how to create life on purpose by tapping into the power of their unconscious mind and marrying the Law of Attraction with everyday practical strategies so they can have more money, more time and more joy — the easy way.

After she met me, she realised that although she was teaching people how to get themselves into vibrational alignment, she hadn't considered that her home needed it too. As it made perfect sense to her, she came on board.

Before doing so she'd noticed unease in her children and, although her business was good, it felt like hard work. She was secretly blaming her husband for things being harder than she knew they needed to be.

What happened when she joined the Feng Shui world?

> *"When I do things, I do them full out. So I went for it, and I did every single thing you told me to do. We went out. We got all of the remedies and put them in straight away. I'm really lucky that I've got a super-supportive partner and it's been epic! The shifts have been epic!*
>
> *I'm fairly sensitive to energy anyway, so I could feel everything shifting.*

The energy in the home shifted, and I thought, that's nice, and if that's all I get out of it, I'm happy.

My husband had been running our finance business since I stepped out to run my business a year before. Suddenly it went crazy and he's had the biggest period for probably the last two or three years. He's done it all on his own, everything just flowed. He's got some amazing backup support that he's found, who are fantastic. And this was after having our main support person go on maternity leave and thinking, 'what are we going to do?' So, it's been amazing!"

Miriam's own business did brilliantly as well and doubled once she'd put all the Feng Shui remedies in place, and then tripled the next month. And she found it easy to do while feeling more relaxed and more in flow. Her family were much more relaxed after the changes were implemented too and family life became more harmonious.

"It's like somebody plucked a pebble out of the pipe that was blocking the flow, and now it's just gushing!"

CHAPTER 17

The Fame and Reputation Area

The south Power Centre of your home is your fame, reputation, and recognition area. This is about how you share your light with the world.

To clarify, this is not just about getting on TV! Some clients have remarked in the past that this area doesn't matter too much because they "don't want to be famous". Don't be fooled. This is a powerful area in so many ways. It is much more about how people recognise you, refer to you, and talk about you. It's someone saying, "Oh she's such a lovely person. She's so helpful. She's so genuine." Absolute miracles can happen for people who have energised this space in terms of their fame and reputation, such as being featured in newspapers, being on TV, becoming well-known, or receiving accolades for what they do.

So, how do you want to be recognised? How do you want people to refer to you? What do you want people to say about you?

Enhancements

- Energise, show off, and display your current achievements
- Put up diplomas and certificates
- Amplify whatever it is that you want to be seen or acknowledged for
- Add a spiritual statue of Brigid, the Irish sun goddess, representing how you shine your light in the world
- Place an object that represents how you share your light with the world, for example, a replica Oscar, a replica Golden Globe, a local newspaper clipping, an image of a sports trophy you want to win, or an affirmation about winning a specific prize
- Display photos of friends or people you admire, whose status you desire
- Add images of people enjoying themselves, achieving what you want to achieve, or appearing excited about their profession.

If you do not wish to display these symbols of admiration overtly, do so discreetly. Nobody needs to know you have set these intentions.

One of my PowerHouse students followed these suggestions and went on to win the highest accolade ever in her career. She entered a contest for two different awards. Then out of the blue, she won Best Overall Service. She was absolutely blown away. Likewise, hanging my

Feng Shui certificates in my fame and reputation area has made a huge difference to my business success.

Affirmations

"I am respected, admired, and appreciated for the work I do."

"I have wonderful relationships with clients and I am grateful for these."

"I am recognised for my skills, talents, and accomplishments."

"I am acknowledged by others for being a loving, caring partner."

"I share my light, my talents, my gifts, and I earn an abundant living."

Talmar's Story

Talmar works with entrepreneurs and business owners on the hiring process and managing best strategies.

When she started working with me she was frustrated and felt like she wasn't a strong enough example for her son in the way she projected and took care of herself. She felt that she and her husband didn't have the cash they wanted, and although they both had businesses, they were not where they wanted them to be.

"So I was working on all kinds of different things, and Feng Shui was something I have always pursued, but just never with a mentor. As soon as I was able to connect with Patricia I was thrilled, because she was totally in line with what I had always wanted to be working with.

The very first cure I remember, was in our master bedroom, our career sector. We needed to add fire that year. So, I went out and I just bought a brand new comforter for the bed. I mean, of all the easy things to change!

So, I go out there, and with intention, I put in my new comforter. Nothing very expensive. I put it on the bed and, within 24 hours, my husband, who's a construction guy, got a call about a big job!

When you do the cures in the house, it works for the whole family. So, within the same twenty-four hours my son got accepted into a free programme that's worth about seventy thousand US dollars over seven years — a free scholarship programme for Japanese immersion.

> **And then, I landed a brand-new client, and I was like, 'Is it really just a comforter?' But, it was!"**

Their house was good for people but bad for money, and once they implemented the specific remedy, things started to turn around.

Talmar was happy but felt her reach in her business was still too small and wanted to focus on the Fame and Reputation area in her house.

> **"Because I wanted to manifest visibility, not only did my business get more clients, more awareness, and more speaking gigs, but I'm now featured on a television show that is about my business. It's going to last through nine months' worth of internet, TV, and all different kinds of places!"**

And the main thing she's learned?

> **"Feng Shui allows the universe source to bring it more easily, more quickly, and bigger than you could ever, ever imagine, so don't limit yourself."**

CHAPTER 18

The Love and Relationships Area

The southwest Power Centre, or area, represents love, marriage, and relationships. While, of course, this area is devoted to your main love relationship, which may be a marriage, be mindful that it is about relationships in your life. This means not only the health of the relationship you have with your partner but also looking after how you relate to others more broadly.

This is important because it means this area may need a little TLC to make sure all the relationships in your life look the way you want them to. If you're struggling to get along with people, the work you do in this Power Centre will revolve around adding in whatever item makes you feel happy and uplifted when you see them. That feeling will be mirrored in your relationships.

Enhancements

- Place an object that represents love to you
- Add in two rose quartz hearts, a pair of mandarin doves, or some peonies, which are lovely in the summertime
- If you are married and you want to enhance your relationship with your husband, get a picture of the two of you on your wedding day or from a happy time when you were dating
- If you are single and want to attract love into your life, add items that represent what you want, including a vision board for who you're attracting
- If you are not married, you can add a picture of you as a couple on a day where you have happy positive memories
- Sink into the positive energy you get from these memories
- When adding anything, make sure it represents being in a couple
- Add images of you doing activities as a couple, such as dancing, drinking wine together, or walking hand-in-hand at the beach
- Find a spiritual statue of Quan Yin, the goddess of love and compassion, the angels, or cupid

Note: Think in pairs! Avoid having pictures of other people (including family photos) or singular items (such as a boat on an ocean or a single woman) in your love and marriage area.

Affirmations

"I experience happy, healthy, loving relationships."

"My perfect partner is kind, patient, and loving."

"My partner and I are experiencing a deeply loving and mutually respectful, fulfilling relationship that has good communication, passion, and joy."

"I only attract loving, healthy relationships into my life."

"All my relationships are healthy, healed, and whole. I experience an abundance of love within my life."

Joanne's Story

Joanne is a small business manager who assists start-ups with their admin needs.

When she joined the PowerHouse programme, she was in a bad place financially, and not sleeping. With bills coming out of her ears, and nothing working, she knew something needed to change. She started going through her house, with the report, day by day adding something new and it started to work for her.

She was in a long-term relationship at the time too, but it wasn't what she wanted or felt she deserved, as it felt one-sided. Feng Shui helped to end her relationship after she created a vision board for love and relationships with pictures of loving couples and buzzwords like passion, love, engagement, and wedding. But within a month she met the love of her life, and a month after meeting, he proposed, they moved in together, bought a house, and booked an overseas trip for Christmas!

Joanne found her dream job and now loves going to work.

> ***"Everything shifted. Completely shifted. I know if it hadn't been for Feng Shui it wouldn't have happened. No way! I would still be stuck in a rut, miserable, sick, and depressed. And I can only thank Feng Shui for [the change]!"***

Joanne believes she is a different person now than who she was twelve months ago.

> ***"I've found myself again. I'm happy, I'm content. I'm more than happy now just to throw things out. I don't need them. They're gone! Yeah. It's so worth doing. It's probably one of the first things I've done and committed to and gone all the way through doing it to the point I got my new house."***

CHAPTER 19

The New Beginnings, Creativity, and Fertility Area

The west Power Centre of your home represents creativity, children, fertility, your inner child, and new beginnings. This area is all to do with what you want to birth.

There are many aspects to this area, so you must ensure that you tune in to the ones you wish to enhance the most. That may be about fertility in the literal sense if you want children. Equally, it may be spending more time with children or bringing a more creative, playful, child-like quality to your life.

So, what do you want to create? How do you want to express your creativity? Do you want to have children? Do you want to express that inner child? What new things do you want to bring into the world?

Enhancements

- Place pictures of children, creative artwork, or symbols of creativity in this area
- Keep your art supplies here, especially if you wish to express more creativity
- Scatter seeds into a bowl and place it in this Power Centre to symbolise new beginnings
- Add a bowl of white Jordan almonds, pomegranate images, or a bowl of pomegranates to represent abundant fertility
- Put up artwork that you enjoy
- Place visuals to represent any creative or writing retreats you wish to attend
- Include objects or images that inspire you
- Include a spiritual statue for the goddess of creativity, Saraswati, and/or Lakshmi, the goddess of abundance and fertility

Affirmations

"I welcome new beginnings and trust in the divine process of life."

"I see myself expressing my creativity easily and in many ways. For this, I am grateful."

"I see myself opening up to experience my creative energies in new, exciting ways."

"I trust that I am a creative being. I allow the divine process to work through me."

"I see my children living their lives to their fullest potential, being healthy, creative, and expressing their natural talents, gifts, and skills. I am grateful for this."

This last affirmation is specifically about bringing positivity to your children.

Andrea's Story

Andrea is a member of our PowerHouse Members Community and lives in a small town in the UK. She says that where she lives, there isn't much everyday talk about these magical opportunities that can occur in peoples' lives. However, she'd seen a few posts from friends of hers who had worked with Feng Shui, and felt inspired by the opportunity to try something new.

> *"I started by creating a vision board — what do I actually want?*
>
> *My number one thing was that I wanted to manifest money. I realised that I had to become worthy of a promotion. I wanted a job where I would be appreciated. I wanted X amount of money per year, a good work-life balance, and I wanted to feel worthy to receive a promotion.*

> *So I put my affirmation in my career corner and thought to myself, "I'll just trust it."*

After joining our PowerHouse programme, Andrea added the remedies to her home and started doing the work. She kept up with her daily meditations, and kept decluttering and connecting with her home.

> *"Then, when I was on holiday in Thailand, and just enjoying being present, I got an email from work saying that there was an opportunity to pay me redundancy. And I was like, Oh, that doesn't go with my goal of wanting a promotion for X amount of money. However, I had a feeling like I should take the redundancy package, even though it went totally against my vision.*
>
> *The redundancy went through, and I was basically unemployed."*

After taking the redundancy package, Andrea could have easily felt discouraged, unsure, and deflated about the direction everything seemed to be going. However, she didn't give up and something amazing happened.

> *"My dream job just appeared in front of me. It met the salary that I wanted. It came with a company car. It came*

with the work-life balance I wanted so that I could work from home. It was literally exactly what I had asked for, so I applied for the job.

My logical mind started getting in the way — telling me that I wasn't good enough — so I was like, right, come on now, do the meditations and trust.

As I continued to trust the process, I ended up getting the job and almost tripled my salary, which would have probably taken me 1015 years to get to in my previous company that gave me the redundancy package."

And Andrea didn't stop there. She kept going! Everything on her vision board, from having passive income to amazing relationships with her husband and kids, she ended up manifesting.

I asked Andrea what her main takeaway was from all that she experienced when working with her vision board and her Feng Shui remedies.

"For me, it's all about trust. I would rec-ommend to anyone to just absolutely; Don't Doubt. Just go for it. What's the worst that could happen? Trust the process. Don't panic. Believe it will happen for you."

CHAPTER 20

The Helpful People and Travel Area

Your home's northwest Power Centre, or area, speaks to helpful people and travel, the capacity to go places, and to be supported. This area concerns everything to do with receiving and allowing support. It is also about direction and your capacity for expansion.

What countries do you dream of visiting? What travel would you like to do? Where else do you want or need to go? Where do you want to take your business or career? What helpful people would you like in your life? Would you like a new cleaner, a babysitter, a DIY person, a virtual assistant, more friends, or a care assistant? Is there any help you need in your life right now? This area gives you permission to dream about all the support you could ever imagine having in your life and just welcome it in.

Enhancements

Sometimes when I am doing Feng Shui consulting, the answer is staring us right in the face. A few years ago, I worked with a woman who wanted to travel to Switzerland. When I was introduced to her home, I saw she had a cuckoo clock. Immediately, I moved her cuckoo clock to her travel Power Centre to anchor the energy of that country in the space. You, too, can think of symbolic items to use as anchors for the places you want to travel.

- Hang artwork of places you love or want to visit
- Add a globe, atlas, travel books, or articles about wherever you wish to travel
- Collect magazines or brochures from travel agents and put them in this space
- Write 'job descriptions' for the helpful people you are calling in
- Make an all-travel vision board
- Put up photos of yourself on holiday in the place you want to go back to
- Add spiritual statues of angels for a sense of having someone watching over you and supporting you, and/or Ganesh, the remover of obstacles

Lastly when it comes to support, trust that all will unfold perfectly for your highest good. The right people will show up at the right time. The right support will materialise if you let it. You don't need to know-how. You only have to set your intention to have what you desire.

Years before I moved to Bali, I was sitting at home in Ireland thinking about how much there was to take care of in the house. It was a large house with so much to manage. I remember saying. "We could do with a house manager. I would just love a house manager." Of course, at that time in my life, people looked at me and said, "You're crazy." But the intention was set!

When we lived in Bali, I took on a house with my husband Ken, and it is normal to have a house manager. Our house manager looks after every detail. She buys light bulbs when we need them and replaces them. She organises the electrician to come when we need one. Now in Greece we have one too. She looks after it all. And this just happened.

Set the intention and then practise non-attachment. As long as you allow something to happen, it can simply flow in.

Affirmations

When writing your affirmations and planting your seeds of intention for this area, imagine you have all the money in the world and there are no obstacles to achieving what you call in. What help would you have if money was no object? Where would you go if you had all the money in the world to travel wherever you liked?

"I accept that which I choose to experience in my life, having an abundance of helpful people to help me whenever the need arises. I am grateful for this."

"I have an abundance of supportive people in my life."

The remaining beautiful affirmations are to anchor in the places where you want to travel, what you want to do there, and what support you need to get there. Have fun with them!

"I have the means to travel abroad whenever I want."

"I happily travel where I choose and have unlimited resources to do so."

"I consciously embark on an amazing sentient journey."

"The right people come to me at the right time to help me get to my next step in an easy, graceful, joyful manner."

"I travel graciously and when I choose. I live the life of my dreams."

Tina's Story

Tina is a PowerHouse member who transformed her family home into her dream home. She turned a home that most people wouldn't bother putting the work into, from feeling heavy and dense to a heavenly oasis.

"I bought my house from my parents, so it was my childhood home and it had stale energy. When I got my Feng Shui report for my home, it was bad for people, bad for money. This was not shocking to me because the moment my parents left the house and moved to Florida, they became much happier and got along really well. It was obvious that the house they had lived in for so long was not supportive of them.

It was clearly bad for money because right before I got the house, a tree fell on it. I can't make this up! Also, the air conditioning just died. So it was like $20,000 worth of damage that I had to pay before I was even living there."

That is wild. So what happened, what turned your home around?

"So I joined the PowerHouse programme and started putting the remedies into my home.

Around that same time, I walked out of my job. I realised that I just couldn't work there anymore. And I ended up finding a better job with a significant increase in income, and a better working environment.

After working with Feng Shui, it's like a completely different house. I have friends over and they say, "Oh my gosh, can I just stay here forever? The energy in your home is so supportive and light and friendly."

So, you obviously love Feng Shui, and it sounds like you did all the work in order to make your home work for you. What else have you enjoyed about being part of the PowerHouse programme?

"The community that Patricia has put together is extremely supportive. It's a community of like-minded people who are all aligning with a state of abundance. It can really help you change your mindset. You can change your house, but you also need to change your mindset. And doing both just helps you grow exponentially. It really is like acupuncture for your home."

PART 4

Feng Shui Room by Room

CHAPTER 21

Best Practices

By energising the areas of your home with the enhancements in Part Three, you will experience powerful shifts. No doubt you have already noticed some of your intentions manifesting. As always with Feng Shui, there are more layers to uncover.

In this section, we will be moving from the Power Centres that you've mapped to looking at the specific rooms of your home and what they symbolise in Feng Shui. This is because, while every house is different in terms of where the Power Centres are going to be, there are some best practices in each room that are going to remain constant for all. For example, perhaps the bedroom of your house is in your prosperity and abundance area, but the bedroom of your neighbour's house is in their helpful people and travel area. Specific recommendations would differ for each, but there are some best practices for bedrooms that you both could implement. That's what we are doing here.

This section is packed with actions and tips to take your home to the next level. There are also hints on what to look out for that may be draining the energy of your home (and life) that you can tackle from a practical perspective. It's not just about decluttering and cleaning, although this will come into play as it always does. It is also about being mindful of what you bring into certain spaces.

Some spaces in your home have powerful associations. What you do with the entrance makes a huge impact on your life overall, as it's where the energy, or *chi,* enters. What you keep in the bedroom will affect the way you rest, relax, and experience intimacy and romance. And what goes on in the kitchen will influence your ability to nourish yourself. So beyond looking at the areas of your home as per the Feng Shui floor plan, the function of each room is an important source of information.

Let's take a look at some Feng Shui best practices one room at a time. For each room, there are so many steps you could take, so I invite you to take your time, note each and every step, and make a checklist of what needs to be tweaked. You can bring other people on board for this journey too. As you Feng Shui your home, you don't want to be feeling overwhelmed. Tackle one job at a time and call in helpful people to whom you can delegate. That's what it's all about.

CHAPTER 22

Entrances

Why do we focus so much on the front door and entrance in Feng Shui? Well, remember when we compared your house to a person? The mouth corresponds to the front door, which is where the energy or *chi* comes in. This is how you feed the home. And, as such, it's crucial to keep this area vibrant, alive, energetic, and incredibly attractive. Not to mention, you must *use* your front door!

Welcoming in

In many cultures, it's normal to not use the front door of a home. I've encountered people who don't even have a front door key and always use another entrance. This is not the path to positive energy for your home, because it blocks the ability of the energy to enter. The idea is to **welcome the energy** instead. So, how do you do this?

Use your front door to come and go from your house. See this area with new eyes. Pretend you're arriving at your house for the first time. Notice what you see and experience. Start right outside, at the front gate, and move through the experience of arriving, as if you were a new person entering. Make it a journey that says, "welcome, welcome, welcome", the whole way along.

The energy is opening here. To allow the chi to flow in, make sure there are **no obstacles**. Declutter outside your front entrance and keep it clear of obstacles, whether it's a step or a front porch. Cut back any looming plants or vines, clear away old newspapers, and make sure bikes and toys are put back in their right place, rather than left cluttering the way in. Clear away any cobwebs, broken or cracked ornaments, dead plants, or weeds. Remove anything at the front of the house that limits the amount of energy entering your home. It's important to make sure that it is nice and open.

Set the mood for what to expect inside by starting that experience outside. Make the area look inviting. Add a welcome mat or sign that signifies, "Come on in. Welcome to our home! We can't wait to have you."

Clean your front door and make sure it's gleaming. If you have old door knockers, doorbells, or doorknobs, make sure they shine.

Finding you

Hang a house number or name, so that it is easy **for the energy to find its way** to your home. Have a clear sign at the front of your home and make sure it looks nice so that it's not something you just pass by or forget about. Sometimes we don't even notice something like a sign or a welcome mat, and they are taken for granted, but it's part of making sure the energy is welcomed in.

Check that your doorbell is working, so that you can **hear who's coming**. Wash your windows too, because this is how you **see who's coming**.

Easy access

Check that the hinges, locks, and handles are working on the door so that it **opens fully and easily**. Ensure your front door doesn't scrape the floor or creak as it opens. While you are doing this, make sure you clear anything that is behind the door that might be stopping it from opening fully. Make sure the energy can flow in with ease.

Likewise, ensure the front gate is **in working order**. A squeaky front gate depletes your energy and is disconcerting to visitors.

Along the path, remove any weeds and dead leaves. Trim shrubbery and bushes along the driveway. Sweep away debris from the doorway as necessary. Mow your front lawn if you have one.

Feeling secure

Check that doorknobs, locks, and hinges are **completely secure**. This security measure cures frustration and anxiety. When a front door is not in good working order, both secure and easily opened, it signifies a struggle or frustration in life.

What's inside?

After setting the expectations for a welcome arrival, stepping inside should feel inviting too. Is the entrance to your home an inviting space?

Reflect on the arrival or take a photo so you can see plainly what vibe the entrance to your home is giving off. Here are some questions to consider. What do you think a visitor can expect inside from the look of your entrance? Is there room for guests to put their shoes? Is there space for visitors' jackets, scarves, and gloves? Are there items from last season still on display? What inviting touches can you add? Is the hallway bright and open? What is the first thing you see when you open your front door?

Remove any mirrors that you can see when entering the front door. Mirrors in entrance ways are a big no-no because energy entering the home is reflected right back out again. All the effort you put into welcoming the *chi is wasted* when it bounces back out, so be mindful of what you place in the entrance area so that it continues to invite the energy in. However, note that it is okay to place mirrors on a side wall.

CHAPTER 23

Bedrooms

Turning to the feel of your bedroom. It is key to dedicate this space to sleep and intimacy, reflecting a relaxing and rejuvenating environment. Essentially, the words to associate with the bedroom of your home are *rest, romance, and relaxation*.

Powerful positioning

The better rested you are, the stronger you will be and the better able to look after your body and support your family. To make sure you get the best rest, let's look at the way your bed is positioned.

Ideally, when considering where to situate your bed, it should feel safe, you should feel loved, and it should ensure you're in a commanding position in your bedroom. Typically, this means being in the space farthest from the door, with a wall behind you, but still able to see the doorway as you lie in bed. In addition, try to avoid the doorway coming straight in at your feet or head.

Now, 90% of the bedrooms I have ever seen or slept in, are designed for the bed to go on one wall, and one wall only. If you're lucky, there might be a second option, or the bedroom may already be set up so that the bed is in the best position, as I've just described. However, if it's not and you can't possibly move the bed to a better place in the room, it will have to stay where it is. Fear not! There are remedies and quick fixes to improve the way your bed position impacts your rest and relaxation.

Having your head to the wall while you're in bed is a good start. If the door is not totally facing you, that is even better. However, if you can't see the door, put a small mirror — that all-powerful Feng Shui tool — at the end of your bed or on a small cabinet, so that you can see the reflection of the door when lying in bed. It's important that you're not reflecting any energy out of the door with the mirror, but rather that you can see the door opening and see who's entering, even if it's just out of the corner of your eye. Doing this gives you a firmer sense of security and safety.

If a mirror is not an option and the head of the bed is the first thing you see when walking through the door, put a strong lamp on a side table to block the chi from coming straight at your head.

Supporting you and your best rest

Wood is the best material for your bed and it should be strong, ideally with a solid headboard. A good headboard is a must, as it gives you a sense of being supported. This is important for quality sleep because you are in this position, asleep, for many hours every night. Again, solid wood is a good material for headboards. Even upholstered headboards are recommended because they are a good combination of soft and strong, which blends the **sense of security** with the feeling of sanctuary.

Any style of bed works, as long as there is **breathing room under the bed**. That means no storing stuff underneath it! Anything under your bed affects the underbelly of your life, so avoid storing unusual items here. I have seen people store all sorts of things under their beds, including broken computers, old shoes, and gifts from ex-partners. Clear out the area under your bed and leave it empty, otherwise, you may find your sleep disturbed. If you do have storage drawers, make sure you don't store anything in them that holds emotive energy. I suggest towels, sheets, linen, or pyjamas — anything that has low-intensity vibrational energy.

Allow free space under the bed and avoid beds that are low to the ground, because these are negative in Feng Shui terms. Dust underneath the bed regularly.

Representing relaxation

Speaking of that word 'sanctuary', frame your thinking about your bedroom in terms of relaxation. Does your bedroom represent rest, romance, and relaxation? If it doesn't, it's time to honour the space where you get your rest, sleep, and have intimate relations with your partner. It is a significant space for you, so it's crucial to **create a sanctuary**. When you come in, you should feel like you can't wait to get into bed and fall asleep. You'll have a great night's sleep because of that feeling.

Switching off

Ensure all work-related items, computers, TV, electronics, and exercise equipment, are in another room.

Having a desk in your bedroom can blur the lines between work and sleep, indicating unclear boundaries and an inability to switch off. If there is no alternative place to put your desk, put a cloth or a shawl over it at night, or when you've finished using it, to clarify those boundaries between working and resting.

If you can't live without a TV, or your partner doesn't want to get rid of the TV from the bedroom, cover it while you sleep.

Like work, exercise equipment represents a feeling of exhaustion, so you don't want to see that as you're falling asleep either.

Clear your nightstand of clutter, including most books. Bear in mind that the bedroom is a place of rest, romance, and relaxation, so it is not the place for a whole library of books to be. Books carry a great deal of energy, information, and charge, which affect your sleep if stored in the bedroom. If you have nowhere else to keep your books, put them inside a cupboard or wardrobe, or ensure the books aren't on display towards you while you're in bed. The idea is that the high energy of books is not in your face and actively affecting your sleep.

Keep your windows clean and replace burnt-out light bulbs, which signify burnout. Anywhere you see light bulbs burning out regularly, take a good look at that area in your life, because it indicates something going on with the energy that needs tending to.

Overhead

Another aspect of creating a feeling of safety in the bedroom is ensuring nothing is hanging overhead.

This means pictures hanging over your bed because they could fall or feel unsafe, even if on a strong nail. Hang pictures on the opposite wall, so you can see the images.

Likewise, make sure there are no exposed beams above your bed. Of course, every house has beams above the ceilings, so covered beams are not the issue here.

However, if there is a sense of something over your head, anything that could fall, or storage units that go over the bed, these will need to be addressed.

For exposed beams, you can soften them by putting up some fabric, soft drapes, or cloth. In some parts of the world, you might have mosquito nets, for example.

For overhead beams that line up with the centre of the bed between you and your partner, consider moving the bed or swapping rooms, because this can be damaging for relationships.

For overhead storage, empty out shelves so that you don't encourage added pressure coming down on top of you.

Calming colour

When creating a sanctuary, colour makes a real difference. The best colours for bed linen are neutral tones like white and creams. Combine these tones with colours you love in the décor of your bedroom, keeping the overall ambience calm. Bear in mind also that pillows, duvets, and sheets should feel luxurious.

Creating harmony

Feng Shui is based on the five elements that are the powerful forces of nature: water, fire, earth, wood, and metal. It's important to understand how balancing these creates harmony. Water affects emotions, which is why I suggest minimising this element in the bedroom so that you get a restful sleep. Remove images containing waterfalls or bodies of water from beside your bed.

Imagery in the bedroom is crucial to **reflect loving relationships**.

If you are in a relationship, add in a stunning photo of yourself together with your partner. Choose one that sparks joy, such as a memory of an amazing day together, like your wedding day or your first date. The image should make you feel incredible, so that each time you see it, you think, "I love that picture of us."

Furthermore, it is not helpful to have pictures of other people (family members, children, or friends) in the bedroom, because you don't want people watching you in bed. It is not recommended to have holy pictures, altars, spiritual statues, or images of a single person, single boat, or single heart in your bedroom.

If you are single and want to attract love, add a picture of a couple doing something that you would love to be doing with a partner. The image should spark joy and inspire you.

Attracting love

Along with harmony and caring for yourself, your bedroom is about attracting a loving relationship. Keeping it neat and organised signals that you are ready to call in a partner.

When I lived in Dublin and was looking for love, I would leave my bedroom door open during the day. The people who passed by could see how much I loved it. I loved my linen. I loved my floor rugs. I loved the pictures on the walls. I was happy with that room and in that room. It was immaculate. It was my sanctuary.

Making your bed in the morning before leaving your bedroom is an **act of self-care** for yourself as well as your home. Dust and vacuum regularly. Hang up clothes. Put away any items you don't need to use right now. Taking **good care of your sanctuary space** indicates that you love it and you are proud of the way you take care of yourself.

Keep your towels in your bathroom, not the bedroom. Especially if they are damp, as they will **dampen the energy** in that bedroom space.

Store suitcases in the attic or garage, not in your bedroom, because this impacts your ability to settle in. Having suitcases under the bed or in the wardrobe may invite a sense of moving again.

If your focus is attracting the right relationship into your life, make space for this person in your bedroom and in your life. Declutter your wardrobe and clear out anything to do with ex-partners and past relationships, gifts from exes, and items of clothing that you may have worn on dates. Organise your closet and drawers. Get spare hangers for your wardrobe and make space on shelving. Make sure you have a pair of nightstands, but I recommend leaving one completely empty for your soulmate.

The position of the bed becomes relevant here again. If you wish to attract a relationship into your life, a single bed is not going to invite that in. Aim for a queen-size bed if you can. The width of a king or super-king-size bed can indicate a lot of space in the relationship. Make sure your bed is not pushed up against the wall on one side. This can be negative for single people because it shows you are not making space for the other person and are 'pushing away love'. Literally, there is no room for another person to get into your bed.

Talking mirrors again, ensure there are no mirrors facing the bed so that you can't see yourself reflected when lying in bed. This is particularly important if you are single and are working on attracting a relationship because the universe sees that there are already two people in the bed, you and the reflection. Avoid mirrors facing the bed and over your head.

Lastly, if you are hoping to attract love, think about adding in a pair of fresh pink peonies. These are flowers that represent abundant love. You should also avoid having live plants in there.

Thinking in pairs

Since imagery is so important in the bedroom, be mindful of the pairings you introduce to this space. Use your whole home like a vision board of your dreams and intentions, making sure the pictures you are hanging up reflect what you want to welcome into your life. What do you want to welcome in?

Think in pairs, but take great care. As you can see from the example of the mirror opposite the bed, it's not as simple as just doubling up on everything. You may have heard all sorts of ideas, like having a second toothbrush, or an empty bedside table. These are indicative of inviting in a love partner. On the other hand, avoid any images of a single woman on her own looking at you, because that is essentially what you are manifesting.

Ideally, thinking in pairs looks like this:

If you're in a relationship, having a queen-size bed and two nightstands with two lamps of equal size, ensures everything is matched and harmonious. However, on your nightstand, make sure you only place items that are relevant to you and your relationship status right now.

If you are calling in a relationship, find an image of love that feels good for you and put it up in your bedroom.

It may be a beautiful statue of a couple dancing, a pair of rose quartz love hearts, affirmations and intentions for your soulmate. Whatever you choose, make sure it reflects what you want to bring into your life, and bedroom!

Michelle's Story

Michelle is a registered nurse and real estate agent in Boston, Massachusetts. She was recently divorced and her kids are college age, so she has begun thinking about the next stage of her life and how she'd like to spend her time.

When she started her journey with Feng Shui, her college-aged boys were still living at home.

> *"I started to add remedies to my home, and then in each of my sons' bedrooms. Obviously, they're in college and both are big college football players. So you can imagine they're like, 'What are you doing?'*
>
> *I said, 'Just don't touch them. You can dust them, but don't touch them.'*
>
> *They're like, fine Mum, whatever.*

We did that in January, and by February 1, Michael, my son who is in college, won $67,000 in the lottery. My sons all said to me, 'Mum, Michael never wins anything, it's your feng shui.' That was just unbelievable and he was able to use it to pay off his undergrad. It was just amazing."

When Michelle joined the PowerHouse programme, she used Feng Shui to help her move into a new home once her boys moved out on their own.

"My dream was to be near the water. I didn't know if I could afford it, but that was my dream. Would you believe that within a few months of joining the programme, I found my home by the water and when I got my report, it said that it is good for money, and good for people. I was ecstatic."

This is just the best story about doing the work and reaping the rewards. Is there anything you'd recommend to people who are interested in joining the course?

"Just believe and trust. Do the programme. Whatever you put in, you'll get back a hundredfold.

The PowerHouse team is amazing. Your team gets back to people, almost immediately with answers to everyone's queries. The PowerHouse team offers a great service.

It's changed my life."

CHAPTER 24

Children's Bedrooms

Feng Shui for children's bedrooms has its own special best practices to bear in mind, so they deserve a dedicated chapter of their own.

Children's bedrooms are about creating a connection between family and children, so add family photos, particularly any photos from a day that was positive and amazing, when everyone got on well. Positive family pictures are highly affirming for children, both in the bedroom and, if you have a two-storey home, along the staircase where the kids walk up to bed.

Avoid bunk beds in children's rooms if you can, because the child sleeping underneath can feel limited and lacking in personal space, as though someone is coming down on them, and the child on top has a sense of disconnection from being far up from the earth. There is also a risk of falling or having difficulty getting down.

Now, in some homes, bunk beds may seem like the only option. If the house is small and you have no more space, bunk beds are a temporary solution, because the children have to have a space to sleep! Longer-term, try to find another answer.

Children's pictures and décor should be appropriate to their age. Tidy away and organise children's toys, avoiding lots of exposed shelving in the bedroom. Wicker baskets and storage bins are better than having toys on display.

Even though this may be unpopular with older children, ensure there are no large electronics, computers, or exercise equipment in their bedrooms. Get the kids to put away electronics in a cupboard at night for sensible boundaries around work and disconnection from that switched-on energy while they sleep.

CHAPTER 25

Kitchens

Kitchens are connected to nourishing your life energy, particularly with wonderful smells and tastes. Even though your kitchen may not be aligned with your prosperity Power Centre, according to your marked-up floor plan, kitchens are connected with prosperity in the sense that they are the place where you nourish yourself.

Clean and clear

For good nourishment in all meanings of the word, the emphasis is on cleanliness, so the first action to take is tossing out any food that has expired or is no longer needed. Have a decluttering session for your kitchen cupboards and pantry.

Keep your kitchen surfaces clean, organised, and uncluttered. If you are in the habit of having equipment out on display on benches or along cabinets, know that this blocks energy from flowing easily, which may have a huge impact on your wealth. Put away anything you do not use on a regular basis and make sure items have a home.

Given the amount of time you spend in your kitchen and living room, the space should feel calm, happy, and supportive.

Fuelling the prosperity fire

The oven, cooker, and/or stove are connected with prosperity. Not only do you nourish yourself from this place, but it is also related to fire energy, which is about heating and creating fire or drive.

Traditionally, Feng Shui recommends placing a mirror behind your stovetop or hob, so as to double the prosperity. It's your choice how far you go with this. You could choose a beautiful large ornate mirror or a small square mirror tile that can be grabbed from somewhere like Ikea. Some people make the whole splashback behind the stovetop mirrored to really increase that prosperity.

You also want to avoid dowsing the fire element of the stove area with water, so that you aren't dampening that prosperity. If your cooker faces the sink, which is associated with water and putting out fire, you need to counteract that. To do this, adding some wood elements will help generate more fire and adding plant greenery will give something for the water to feed on.

What might this look like? Pop a small green rug on the ground between the cooker and sink. Alternatively, hang a small green tea towel in front of the stove. The idea is to keep the positive energies and make sure they are not depleting each other.

Diverting danger

Although this one is contentious because many people want to be using knives in the kitchen quite frequently, I recommend not having knife blocks on display. In fact, you don't want any dangerous objects out in that area. Put your **knives away** in a drawer. There are some great knife blocks that slide into a drawer easily. Or try magnetic bars inside a cupboard. The main thing is that knives aren't on display.

This particularly impacts the life area that corresponds with your kitchen on your floor plan. For example, if your kitchen is also your love and marriage area, knives could create highly negative energy, as they resemble weapons.

Also, avoid having objects hanging down. Objects overhead can be quite overpowering, as can tall cupboards with lots of cases, items, or ornaments. Avoid storing anything out of reach or too high for you to reach easily, which could be dangerous, and might fall and injure you.

CHAPTER 26

Dining Rooms

Dining room areas are associated with life-giving bounty and with nurturing relationships. This room is where you eat together, where you come together as a family, and where you have memorable occasions.

Bringing people together

Keeping in mind that you need to be practical and do what works for you and your space, I recommend having a round or oval dining table if you can. Symbolically, having soft round edges is ideal, because the intention is to create a space that brings people together to interact lovingly.

When you come to the final section of *The Happy Home* and you discover your four power directions, according to your personal trigram, you can extend the exercise for the whole family or every person who lives in your home. When you have an idea of everyone's best direction, organise them to sit around the table in alignment with their personal trigram.

Multiplying abundance

Add in some symbols of prosperity and abundance, such as fresh flowers or fruit. A bowl of nine oranges is auspicious in Feng Shui because oranges are powerfully associated with more abundance; when you open an orange, there are many more pieces inside.

This is another instance where placing a mirror underneath the bowl will double the amount of positive energy of whatever it is reflecting.

CHAPTER 27

Laundries and Closets

You know where your closets, laundry, and storage areas are located in your home, now that you've mapped out your floor plan. But did you know that your laundry area is also related to prosperity? Once you know that this room of your home is related to money, you'll no doubt be more mindful of how you treat it. Look at that area of your home, see where it is, and commit to being more organised there.

Utility rooms and closets tend to have less impact on your home's energy, so there's no need to spend a great deal of time here. However, that does not mean they don't need to be kept tidy. It is good practice to reduce the amount stored in them on a regular basis, because wherever anything is left in storage for a long time, the energy stagnates, and becomes stuck.

Pay attention to the area of your life that corresponds to this room of your home. Any boxes or piles of stuff just sitting there, stuck there, and never touched, will not be supportive of you. They stagnate the energy, particularly in that part of your life.

CHAPTER 28

Bathrooms

When we consider Feng Shui for bathrooms and toilets, one important factor is in play. Water is about prosperity and abundance, but the bathroom is the place where you **release, cleanse, and let go**. The essence of Feng Shui for bathrooms is therefore ensuring you do not release, cleanse, and let go of your prosperity. How do we tackle this?

Keeping money in

To prevent a loss of abundance, the water element of bathrooms needs to be grounded or earthed.

This means **avoiding the colour blue**, which represents more water. Unfortunately, many bathroom décors are already blue, supposedly because we associate bathrooms with water, the sea, and the ocean. It is an obvious colour choice for decorating, but you should limit it where possible, and consider changing it. If you are decorating now or in the future, avoid it altogether.

You should also **remove any images of water** or anything connected to oceans, rivers, or lakes.

What stops water from being in its fullest flow? Start to think about the earth, about grounding, about slowing water down. If a river was flowing, a dam or river bank would stop the flow and contain the water. It's the same idea for your bathroom. Use pebbles to stop the energy flowing away from your bathroom, by placing one in each corner of the room.

If your bathroom is located in your central Power Centre, **introduce earth tones** into the décor, laundry baskets, or linen. Choose towels that make you think of the earth and grounding when you see them. Select all kinds of earth and nature-related objects for your bathroom.

Keeping **plumbing in excellent order** is vital. If you see the tiniest drip, that means money is dripping away somewhere and abundance is leaving your home.

Keep toilet lids down so your money won't be flushed away. Cover all drains. Shut your bathroom door and keep it closed at all times.

Lastly, it can be effective to tie a piece of red string around the outflow of the taps, such as underneath your sink where the water flows out. The red colour represents fire, which counteracts the water flowing out. This is an auspicious gesture in Feng Shui.

Upwards growth

What can you add to your bathroom to maintain prosperity?

Firstly, keep the bathroom clean and introduce earthy colours. Add plants such as ferns, which love the humidity of a bathroom and grow well there.

To deflect good energy coming into the bathroom and going down the drain, think about placing a mirror on the entrance door to your bathroom. This pushes the chi away, preventing it from leaving the house. This tip comes with a warning. Only do this if your main bathroom is upstairs and not facing the staircase, because of other considerations around using mirrors.

CHAPTER 29

Offices

Applying Feng Shui to your office can vary, depending on whether your office is in your home, or in a separate building, whether you are self-employed or own your own company.

Without getting too complicated, we're going to look at some of the most important things you can implement into any office space.

Clearing the clutter off your desk. This will give you space to breathe and to create. It's really important to do this so that energy flows into your office and your business. Once you start clearing your desk, you'll feel the energy shift immediately. An office filled with clutter leads to overwhelm and anxiety in your business. Having a neat and organised office makes such a big difference.

Your devices count too! Decluttering also includes your computer, and your desktop, removing annual files, deleting anything, unnecessary emails, and getting rid of anything that you do not use right now in your business. If you have old documents, old business ideas, or old businesses that you're not going to run with anymore, maybe it's time to delete them and make space for new opportunities in your business. File away what you need and delete the rest.

Lighting. Make sure you use as much full spectrum light as possible. We spend so much time in our offices, and it's important that our environment supports us. Full-spectrum lighting is powerful in reducing the negative impact of fluorescent or LED light.

Add inspirational colour and artwork. Make sure that the items in your office are comfortable and that they inspire you. You want your office to look like what your business should reflect. Make it into a space of inspiration!

Add plants. Plants are great for creating clean air for your office. Anything that feels uplifting and bright and inspiring will be really good. Bring in plants like ferns or money plants. The energy of plants indicates upward growth, so plants are not only good for your health but support the growth of your business!

Sit in a strong, supportive chair. I cannot reiterate enough having a strong chair that you feel comfortable in. You want to sit in a chair that makes you feel like "I'm the boss."

Have a solid wall behind your back. Your desk position is really important, and you should always have a solid wall behind your back if possible. This is a representation of support and foundation for you in your business. If you don't have a solid wall behind you, you might feel on edge, tense, or totally unsupported.

Create strong, positive affirmations. Add affirmations like, *My business environment nurtures me, my clients, and supports my growth. My business is healthy and growing and vibrant. The universe provides me with an abundance of amazing clients who want to use my services.* Take a little time to journal and write out what is relevant to you, and place these affirmations somewhere in your office.

When Stephen Spielberg hired a Feng Shui consultant to work on his home, the consultant pointed out that the two Oscars he won were positioned on the way to the toilet. She moved the Oscars closer to his office and placed them in his fame and reputation Power Centre. What kind of difference can you imagine this simple placement can make?

PART 5

Powerful Feng Shui for You

CHAPTER 30

Art and Feng Shui

After I moved in with Ken, we were coming to the end of doing up our house. I'd moved everything into the bathroom and was moving everything into the master bedroom from the smaller one where we had been sleeping. At the end of our bed, I left a blank space, because I knew I wanted to find and put up a picture of a couple that sparked joy in me.

A couple of weeks later, I came across a beautiful print of a couple. In the picture, the woman was wearing a red coat and leaning up towards a man in a dark coat, who was holding an umbrella. She was moving in to kiss him. This print reminded me so much of my first date with Ken, even down to the colour of the coat she was wearing — red, my favourite colour. Instantly, I bought the painting, went home, and hung it at the foot of the bed.

Out of nowhere, I began thinking about getting a dog. I had never in my whole life wanted a dog, never had any kind of yearning for one, not even as a kid. I didn't pass any remark, just started noticing that I really wanted a dog, all of a sudden.

Eight weeks later, I was chatting to a neighbour. Out of the blue, she mentioned rescuing a dog she'd found down the road. She'd had to take him to the pound. I was suddenly overcome by her sad story. And in that instant, I knew! "That's it! I want the dog. I'm going to the pound."

Off I went to the pound and found the dog my neighbour had told me about. I adopted him on the spot and named him Marley. I took him home and that was that. I had him in the house. I got used to him being around. I didn't know what, why, or how I ended up with this dog, but I had Marley now and I loved him.

The next day, a friend called over for a tour of the house, now that we'd finished doing up the place. I showed her into the bedroom, pointing out the new bed, the new headboard, everything. She looked up and noticed the picture. Casually, she said, "Oh look, there's you and Marley."

I had not seen the dog in the picture when I bought the print, but there it all was. The woman in the red coat, the red coat identical to my own red coat, was me. And the woman had a little dog, the exact same size, the exact same floppy hair, the exact same curly tail as my new furry friend, Marley. I hadn't known where my urge or desire for the dog came from, but as soon as my friend pointed it out, immediately I saw it there. Every single day for the last few weeks, that picture was there at the end of my bed; a woman in a red coat with a dog. I had seen it every night when I went to sleep, every morning when I woke up. It was there for weeks, entering my subconscious mind. And now, there I was with a new dog.

Art is crazy powerful in Feng Shui.

I can't stress enough the importance of art in the home and its effect on your subconscious mind. Unbeknownst to you, the art you have around you, while you spend all the time you do in your home, impacts what you manifest in your life.

Thankfully for me, my story of the power of artwork was a pretty positive one, but imagine paintings that are not so positive. If you bring something into your life unconsciously — unintentionally — imagine the ramifications that could have.

Art to avoid

Think about what it is that you want to attract into your life, what you've been writing in your affirmations, and what you've been setting intentions for. The images you need in your house must mirror that energy. That means avoiding anything that will drag you down or go against the dreams you have for your life. It also means avoiding anything that will deplete the energy of your home.

- **People sleeping:** Except in the bedroom, avoid pictures of people sleeping
- **Singular items:** If you are single and want to attract love, and even if you are in a relationship, avoid solitary people in pictures. Likewise, avoid images of one flower on its own in a vase, or one boat floating on the ocean. For love, unless the picture sparks absolute joy, think in pairs throughout your whole home
- **Solitary women:** This includes people in relationships. Notice if you have any pictures of single women. This can indicate being in a relationship but spending a lot of time alone or being solitary within a relationship
- **Boats tied up:** These are a sign of going nowhere
- **Stormy scenes:** Imagine what this signifies!
- **Family photos over the fireplace:** The energy of fire resides in the fireplace. Even if the fire is not lit, the intention of the space is fire. The fire element can create tension, so placing a family photo over the fireplace could cause a tense relationship between the people in the home or in the picture

Art is personal

Art is completely personal. Someone might love something. Someone else might hate it. If you love a piece and it sparks joy or has happy memories attached to it, keep it! Just be mindful of the undercurrent of the image, what it signifies, and how others may interpret it.

A Hollywood director was having his office Feng Shui-ed. When the Feng Shui consultant arrived in his office, the first thing she noticed was a massive picture of a gun. As I mentioned earlier in this book, having weapons or knives on display is a big no-no, as it can relate to adversity and tension. And there he was, a Hollywood director, with a huge gun image right there in his office, displayed loud and proud.

The consultant asked, "What does this picture mean to you?" And when he started explaining, the director got so excited, "This was the first movie that I directed. It was *the* biggest success and *my* biggest success." He raved about the movie it represented. And the Feng Shui consultant told him to keep the gun picture.

You see, that picture was not about the gun. To the Hollywood director, that picture was about success. It reminded him of his success, his career, of keeping going, of enjoying the journey, of joy, and of his positive energy.

That's what I mean when I say art is personal. And that's why, when I suggest avoiding some imagery, I'm not telling you to get rid of art you already have. I'm not saying you should go and get rid of all the pictures of sleeping people, single people, boats tied up, or stormy scenes.

First, take note of the name of the painting. Then see where it's hanging in your home. Think about the positioning in your home. Compare that to the area of your life and see how it relates.

Once, I worked with a woman who had a painting in her home called the Tale of the Two Suitors. It showed a woman with two men chasing after her, and it was hanging in her family and community area. At the time she had bought it, she told me, there were two guys in her life.

Art is representative of where you are and what's going on in your life. I am not asking you to get rid of your favourite artwork. Just reflect. Understand that a stormy scene in your prosperity area could make it a rough ride when it comes to wealth. If you've spent a lot of money on paintings or invested in art, make sure that artwork is sparking joy.

What to add

- Happy and positive scenes
- Images that are reflective of the Power Centre where your picture will hang.

CHAPTER 31

Money and Feng Shui

The last aspect of Feng Shui that is important to cover in a beginner's guide like this, is money. It's a layer of Feng Shui that is undeniably potent, where clearing your clutter and being intentional about what you want to call in is paramount.

As you've been working your way through this book, you'll have picked up on some of these tips, but with specific reference to money, it's important to go back through this checklist and make sure nothing is slipping through the cracks.

Keep on cleaning

Remember where I suggested cleaning your windows and front door? These are going to keep getting dirty and will keep needing to be cleaned. If something is not working in your life, and you've gone through this book and done all you can, the entrance of your home may hold the key. It's where you should spend your time if you think you've done all you can. The more effort and energy you spend at the mouth of your home, the more your home will love you, welcome in new energy, and feel that chi entering.

While you clean, express gratitude, because with gratitude comes acknowledgement and appreciation. When you are grateful for what you have already received, you'll notice more. So, give thanks for even the tiniest blessings.

Abundance mindset and love attraction work closely together in Feng Shui. When you have ample money to share, give as generously as you can. When you don't have ample money to share, you can still give some of your time, energy, compassion, appreciation, or gratitude. Give with the power of your thoughts, so that you're able to reap the reward.

Doing this as you're cleaning and decluttering is extra powerful. You may find a penny under your front door mat. You may find ten euros in the pocket of an old jacket that you find in the back of the cupboard when you're decluttering. The more gratitude you express for your home, the more it will give back to you.

Looking for clues

Your home is giving you clues about where you can become more prosperous or stop draining your energy.

Notice which area of your home the bulbs are burning out in and replace them. You may see that these areas are where you are dimming your own energy. There will be something that is exhausting you in that area. Burnt-out bulbs are your home giving you a sign. Think what that sign could mean.

Prosperous plants

Welcome fresh flowers and plants into your home because they represent growth. In Feng Shui, ferns, bamboo, and money plants are particularly wonderful for financial abundance. Lucky bamboo is upward growing and has little twirls or spirals, showing the flow of life. Money plants are succulents that hold on to the water. These are so positive for prosperity and are easy to grow and maintain. Soft ferns can be great too, as they grow upwards — just avoid spiky varieties.

Remove dead plants, dead flowers, dried flowers, and silk flowers, as they represent dead energy. These are not recommended in any Feng Shui, because they are stagnant, hold on to past energy, and have no life around them.

Working order

If you want money flowing in, keep all items around the house working! Broken energy comes from broken stuff, so anything broken, cracked, or chipped that is unable to be repaired, let it go. In particular, replace or fix your office desk or office chair, as those are significant when broken.

Maybe you're having difficulty letting go of something that is broken, cracked, or chipped. If so, find a cord-cutting meditation to help you release it. You can download a meditation from www.patricialohan.com/happyhomebonuses. Try to keep in mind that everything is replaceable, like breathing in and out. At any moment, you are able to inhale and bring in new energy. Then exhale and let it all go. All the time, every moment, new things are coming. All the time, every moment, the old is being let go. Allow yourself to step into that abundant mindset when releasing anything broken, cracked, or chipped if it can't be repaired.

Tighten loose door knobs or handles, and make sure you have handles on your doors. Drawer handles are such tiny little things and easily overlooked, but each time you go to use a frustrating broken handle, it depletes your energy. When you get annoyed trying to open a stuck drawer or use a broken handle, this speaks to you getting a grip on your finances and your life. It's about how you *handle* yourself and anything that comes your way. Repair all door knobs or handles, and make sure they're solid.

Make sure the stove, which represents prosperity, is in good condition. This is a reflection of what's going on in your life.

Keep all plumbing in excellent working order, because even the tiniest leak from a sink or tap represents money dripping away. Fixing it allows more space for abundance.

Keeping abundance in

Cover your drains to keep money in your possession. You can do this by putting stones or pebbles over drains. Of course, the water still needs to flow out somewhere and you don't want your drains totally blocked up, so the water can't flow out. It just needs to not be flowing out at great speed.

Likewise, keep the toilet lids down, so your money won't be 'flushed away', and close toilet doors at all times. It's key that you don't flush the flow of abundance and prosperity out of your house. You want to keep it in your home.

Symbols of money

Balance your accounts regularly. Pay your bills on time. Check your bank accounts as a matter of habit.

Energise your wallet. Make sure your wallet feels luxurious to attract money. Once you have done your personal trigram, which is coming up, you'll know which personal Feng Shui colour you should get a wallet in. Otherwise, use red.

Red is the colour for attracting money, although your personal colour will be far more potent at doing that.

Make sure your wallet is clean, neat, and organised. Check there are no rips or tears. Ask yourself if your wallet sparks joy. You should love your wallet and feel as though you have a safe, happy place for your money. How do you feel when you see your wallet?

Get rid of credit cards, unused bank cards, store cards, details of bank accounts you've closed, and documents associated with those. Streamline your paper documentation and get organised.

Affirmations

"There's plenty more where that came from. I am grateful for that."

"I deserve to be prosperous and wealthy."

"Money flows to me easily."

"Money and prosperity help me to help others."

"The more money I give, the more that I achieve."

"I enjoy being paid well for what I do."

"I'm willing to receive money for my pleasure."

"I'm willing to allow my life to be fun and easy."

All these little money tips will add up to a massive mindset change. You have stepped into the flow of abundance, living generously, sharing the abundant energy you created in your home.

Spending and giving within your means is a powerful last message I want to leave you with. Prosperity flows to you when the energy is moving. So, make sure you maintain the flow of energy — of money — around your happy, healthy, wealthy home.

Susie's Story

Susie has been a member of our PowerHouse community since 2018 and has had amazing success with her home. Susie lives outside of Boston in the USA.

When Susie joined our programme, she was at a pivotal point in her life.

> ***"I was at a place where I had lost my job, had two kids, and was getting***

divorced. This was kind of my Hail Mary, to be honest with you.

Three weeks after joining the programme, after getting my report and starting to implement my remedies, we got a surprise check from the US government. I was like, I was not expecting that much money."

After her divorce, Susie started doing some work on calling love back into her life. She started working with the artwork in her home and aligning the images and symbols in her home with a loving partnership. She reflected on a few paintings in her bedroom that were nice from an interior design point of view, but not great for attracting love.

"Patricia said to me, "Well, what's more important? The paintings or finding love?

I ended up pulling those paintings down.

Then, literally, I put up a beautiful painting that I loved for my bedroom. I put it up and the next morning, my high school sweetheart messaged me on Facebook.

I had messaged him over the Christmas holidays, but he never replied so I kind of gave up on reconnecting. And literally the next day, he contacted me. Now we're dating."

This story just gives me shivers! So, Susie, what is the best advice you can give to people who are interested in joining our community?

"I think the biggest piece is to trust, just having constant faith. It's not just the programme. It's the change in your mindset. I think you just have to have faith. Don't question, just do the work, and get your remedies in. Just do it!"

CHAPTER 32

Personal Trigrams

Personal Trigrams are like your own personal Feng Shui power number. They are completely separate from the Feng Shui of your home.

In Feng Shui, we work with the five elements. This is our biggest philosophy. The elements we work with include fire, water, wood, metal, and earth. So, when you get your personal trigram number, you are going to be one of those elements. Your trigram will have a specific meaning and interpretation, which describes your general nature.

Your personal trigram will tell you a few things. It will tell you what your element is, which colours are your 'power colours', which colours might deplete you, and what are your 'power directions'.

For example, if your trigram number corresponds to the element of water, then you might do well to wear the colour blue, have a blue wallet, or you might enjoy activities that involve water. In essence, the water element is your symbol and where you feel most at home. This is called your 'essence colour'.

Now, what does this mean for you? Basically, using your essence colour is super powerful. It is helping you be more in your element and connect with your energy. It is suggested to wear your essence colours from time to time in order to connect with your element.

It's important to note that these colours are individual to you. They are not the colours for your home. For example, if you are a fire element, and it is suggested for you to wear red from time to time, or have a red wallet, this does not mean that you should paint your home or your bedroom red.

In addition to your essence colours, you are also given colours that "feed" you. For example, let's say you are a wood element. Wood represents anything that is green, such as plants. If you think about the element that a plant needs, you can determine that plants need water. So, if your element is wood, then your essence colour is green, and the colours that feed you would correlate with water.

We often recommend that you don't go overboard with your essence colours and colours that feed you. You don't have to wear these colours every day or change your whole wardrobe. It's more to have an awareness of these colours when you are doing something important like going to an interview, giving a speech, or designing your business logo. One really great way to incorporate one of your colours is to pick a wallet or handbag in either your essence or supporting colour. This is a great way to easily utilise your "power colours" without totally changing your wardrobe.

In addition to your essence colour, and the colour that feeds you, there are also colours that are not recommended, or what we call colours that deplete you.

While these are the recommended colours, again, it is not necessary for you to change your wardrobe, or never wear a colour that depletes you. It's simply about being more mindful of the colours that are supportive for you, and which ones might not be best when engaging in important events and activities.

If you find out your best colours and you think, "But I don't like that colour," that's okay! You don't have to wear it. This is just something for you to play with. It's not the end of the world if you don't want to wear your power colours, but it's helpful to experiment and see how different you feel when you wear your supportive colours.

In addition to recommending colours for you to wear, you can also find out your best personal directions with your trigram. Your best personal directions are usually the direction you have your back to.

For example, you would determine the direction your headboard is facing, the wall behind your office chair, and the wall behind your couch as the directions you are aligned with. As we spend a great deal of time in these three locations, it's a huge bonus if at least one of these locations corresponds to your power direction.

Again, there are so many factors that go into Feng Shui-ing a home. Don't stress if you find out that there's no way for you to place your headboard, office chair, or couch in alignment with one of your best personal directions. It's not the end of the world. If, however, you have the option to do so, and it doesn't compromise the general Feng Shui layout rules for your bedroom, office and living room, then we recommend you choose that option.

You can download the calculations sheet from www. patricialohan.com/happyhomebonuses you will find out how to calculate your own personal trigram, and determine your power colours and power directions.

Trigram Number: 1

- Your Element is **WATER**
- Your Essence Colours are: **Blue & Black**
- The Colours that **DEPLETE** you are: **Earth tones, Browns, Yellows, Cream and Greens**
- The Colours that **FEED** you are: **Gold, Silver, Copper & Grey**
- The Element that **FEEDS** you is **METAL**
- The Elements that **DEPLETE** you are **WOOD** and **EARTH**

- Your qualities are being flexible, yet focused and determined. You are empathetic, artistic and given to deep thought but tend to worry too much and may be overly sensitive.

- **Southeast** (SE) is your Personal Best direction. The best location for Prosperity and Great Fame. Have your back face this direction for productivity. The best location for the main breadwinner of the home to enter in.

- **East** (E) is the best location for Great Health and Good Fortune. Good health location for the parents/elders of the home. Have your back face this direction while eating for better digestion.

- **South** (S) is your best location for Family Harmony, Good Public Relationships and Longevity. Good health direction for the children in the home.

This area improves family relationships and prevents arguments.

- **North** (N) is your best location for Overall Harmony, Clarity (decision-making) and Peace. The best direction to place your headboard (so that the crown of your head faces this direction) to receive a good night's sleep. Good direction to sleep in and to help with fertility.

Trigram Number: 2

- Your Element is **EARTH**
- Your Essence Colours are: **Earth tones, Browns, Yellows, Cream**
- The Colours that **FEED** you are: **Red, Purple, Burgundy, Burnt Orange, Bright Pink**
- The Colours that **DEPLETE** you are: **Green, Gold, Silver, Copper and Grey**
- The Element that **FEEDS** you is: **FIRE**
- The Elements that **DEPLETE** you are: **METAL** and **WOOD**

- Your qualities are that you are very strong (caregivers) and can be a great leader, primarily in earthly matters.

- **Northeast (NE)** is your Personal Best direction. The best location for Prosperity and Great Fame. Have your back face this direction for productivity. The best location for the main breadwinner of the home to enter in.

- **West (W)** is the best location for Great Health and Good Fortune. Good health location for the parents/elders of the home. Have your back face this direction while eating for better digestion.

- **Northwest (NW)** is your best location for Family Harmony, Good Public Relationships and Longevity. Good health direction for the children in the home. This area improves family relationships and prevents arguments.

- **Southwest (SW)** is your best location for Overall Harmony, Clarity (decision making) and Peace. The best direction to place your headboard (so that the crown of your head faces this direction) to receive a good night's sleep. Good direction to help with fertility.

Trigram Number: 3

- Your Element is **Soft Wood**
- Your Essence Colours are: **Greens**
- The Colours that **FEED** you are: **Black and Blue**
- The Element that **FEEDS** you is **WATER**
- The Elements that **DEPLETE** you are **FIRE** and **METAL**

- The Colours that **DEPLETE** you are: **Red, Purple, Burgundy, Burnt Orange, Bright Pink, Gold, Silver, Copper & Grey**

- Your qualities are being generally even-tempered but you can have sudden outbursts. You like to be moving and are not well-suited to a job where you have to sit still for long. You are enthusiastic and can be loud at times.

- **South** (S) is your Personal Best direction. The best location for Prosperity and Great Fame. Have your back face this direction for productivity. The best location for the main breadwinner of the home to enter in.

- **North** (N) is the best location for Great Health and Good Fortune. Good health location for the parents/elders of the home. Have your back face this direction while eating for better digestion.

- **Southeast** (SE) is your best location for Family Harmony, Good Public Relationships and Longevity. Good health direction for the children in the home. This area improves family relationships and prevents arguments.

- **East** (E) is your best location for Overall Harmony, Clarity (decision making) and Peace. The best direction to place your headboard (so that the crown of your head faces this direction) to receive a good night's sleep. Good direction to help with fertility.

Trigram Number: 4

- Your Element is **HARD WOOD**
- Your Essence Colours are: **Greens**
- The Colours that **FEED** you are: **Black & Blue**
- The Element that **FEEDS** you is: **WATER**
- The Colours that **DEPLETE** you are: **Red, Purple, Burgundy, Burnt Orange, Bright Pink, Gold, Silver, Copper & Grey**

- The Elements that **DEPLETE** you are: **FIRE** & **METAL**

- Your qualities are being insightful and often driven but, like the wind's direction, you can change your mind abruptly and often. You tend to be creative and artistic.

- **North (N)** is your Personal Best direction. The best location for Prosperity and Great Fame. Have your back face this direction for productivity. The best location for the main breadwinner of the home to enter is.

- **South (S)** is the best location for Great Health and Good Fortune. Good health location for the parents/elders of the home. Have your back face this direction while eating for better digestion.

- **East (E)** is your best location for Family Harmony, Good Public Relationships and Longevity. Good health direction for the children in the home. This area improves family relationships and prevents arguments.

- **Southeast (SE)** is your best location for Overall Harmony, Clarity (decision making) and Peace. The best direction to place your headboard (so that the crown of your head faces this direction) to receive a good night's sleep. Good direction to help with fertility.

Trigram Number: 6

- Your Element is **Hard Metal**
- Your Essence Colours are: **Gold, Silver, Copper**
- The Colours that **FEED** you are: **Earth tones, Browns, Yellows, Cream**
- The Element that **FEEDS** you is **EARTH**
- The Elements that **DEPLETE** you are **WATER** and **FIRE**

- Your qualities are being a natural-born leader and authority figure. However, you can be headstrong with very strong masculine energy.

- **West (W)** is your Personal Best direction. The best location for Prosperity and Great Fame. Have your back face this direction for productivity. The best location for the main breadwinner of the home to enter in.

- **Northeast (NE)** is the best location for Great Health and Good Fortune. Good health location for the parents/elders of the home. Have your back face this direction while eating for better digestion.

- **Southwest (SW)** is your best location for Family Harmony, Good Public Relationships and Longevity. Good health direction for the children in the home. This area improves family relationships and prevents arguments.

- **Northwest (NW)** is your best location for Overall Harmony, Clarity (decision making) and Peace. The best direction to place your headboard (so that the crown of your head faces this direction) to receive a good night's sleep. Good direction to help with fertility.

Trigram Number: 7

- Your Element is **SOFT METAL**
- Your Essence Colours are: **Gold, Silver, Grey**
- The Colours that **FEED** you are: **Earth tones, Browns, Yellows, Cream**
- The Element that **FEEDS** you is **EARTH**
- The Elements that **DEPLETE** you are **WATER** and **FIRE**

- Your qualities are being artistic, creative, sociable and talkative. You like things done right and you like to lead.

- **Northwest** (NW) is your Personal Best direction. The best location for Prosperity and Great Fame. Have your back face this direction for productivity. The best location for the main breadwinner of the home to enter in.

- **Southwest** (SW) is the best location for Great Health and Good Fortune. Good health location for the parents/elders of the home. Have your back face this direction while eating for better digestion.

- **Northeast** (NE) is your best location for Family Harmony, Good Public Relationships and Longevity. Good health direction for the children in the home. This area improves family relationships and prevents arguments.

- **West** (W) is your best location for Overall Harmony, Clarity (decision making) and Peace. The best direction to place your headboard (so that the crown of your head faces this direction) to receive a good night's sleep. Good direction to help with fertility.

Trigram Number: 8

- Your Element is **Earth**
- Your Essence Colours are: **Earth Tones, Yellows, Browns, Creams**
- The Colours that **FEED** you are: **Red, Purple, Burgundy, Burnt Orange, Bright Pink**
- The Element that **FEEDS** you is **FIRE**
- The Elements that **DEPLETE** you are **METAL** and **WOOD**

- Your qualities are being very stable; however, you can be stubborn. You are very youthful.

- **Southwest (SW)** is your Personal Best direction. The best location for Prosperity and Great Fame. Have your back face this direction for productivity. The best location for the main breadwinner of the home to enter in.

- **Northwest (NW)** is the best location for Great Health and Good Fortune. Good health location for the parents/elders of the home. Have your back face this direction while eating for better digestion.

- **West (W)** is your best location for Family Harmony, Good Public Relationships and Longevity. Good health direction for the children in the home. This area improves family relationships and prevents arguments.

- **Northeast (NE)** is your best location for Overall Harmony, Clarity (decision making) and Peace. The best direction to place your headboard (so that the crown of your head faces this direction) to receive a good night's sleep. Good direction to help with fertility.

Trigram Number: 9

- Your Element is **Fire**
- Your Essence Colours are: **Red, Purple, Burgundy, Burnt Orange, Bright Pink**
- The Colour that **FEEDS** you: **Green**
- The Element that **FEEDS** you is **WOOD**
- The Elements that **DEPLETE** you are **EARTH** and **WATER**

- Your qualities are being extremely active, sometimes to the point of becoming ill or burning yourself out. You are very passionate, however, you can be hot-tempered.

- **East** (E) is your Personal Best direction. The best location for Prosperity and Great Fame. Have your back face this direction for productivity. The best location for the main breadwinner of the home to enter in.

- **Southeast** (SE) is the best location for Great Health and Good Fortune. Good health location for the parents/elders of the home. Have your back face this direction while eating for better digestion.

- **North** (N) is your best location for Family Harmony, Good Public Relationships and Longevity. Good health direction for the children in the home. This area improves family relationships and prevents arguments.

- **South** (S) is your best location for Overall Harmony, Clarity (decision making) and Peace. The best direction to place your headboard (so that the crown of your head faces this direction) to receive a good night's sleep. Good direction to help with fertility.

Find Your Chinese Animal

Download the Personal Trigrams Calculations sheet from www.patricialohan.com/happyhomebonuses and you will get your Chinese Animal too.

Rat: Rat people are popular. They like to invent things and are good artists.

Ox: Ox people are dependable and calm. They are good listeners and have strong ideas.

Tiger: Tiger people are brave. They are respected for their deep thoughts and courageous actions.

Rabbit: Rabbit people are nice to be around. They like to talk and many people trust them.

Dragon: Dragon people have good health and lots of energy. They are good friends because they listen well.

Snake: Snake people love good books, food, music and plays. They have good luck with money.

Horse: Horse people are popular, cheerful and quick to compliment others. They can work very hard.

Goat: Goat people are good artists. They ask many questions, like nice things and are wise.

Monkey: Monkey people are funny. They can always make others laugh and are good problem solvers.

Rooster: Rooster people are hard workers. They have many talents and think deep thoughts.

Dog: Dog people are loyal and can always keep a secret. Sometimes they worry too much.

Pig: Pig people are good students. They are honest and brave. They always finish a project or assignment.

CHAPTER 33

What Feng Shui Consultants Never Share!

Congratulations on making it this far! I am so excited for what will unfold, now that you've been introduced to the basics of Feng Shui. You may already have noticed some small changes as you've started to do this work. You may have even experienced some huge wins as you've gone about your home more intentionally. As I've said throughout *The Happy Home*, doing these basics is incredibly powerful.

Your home is the foundation for everything. When your home's energy is brought back into flow, the rest of your life follows. I hope that, over the course of this book, you have gained clarity and insights into the environment you live in and how it impacts your world. The journey so far, from that old reality you defined when you took stock of the state of your home to the life you are living now full of possibilities, has embraced the power of Feng Shui and you are surely starting to reap the rewards, seeing glimpses of a home that complements your personal and professional intentions.

By now, you understand how to use Feng Shui to transform your home into a happy, healthy and wealthy space, drawing in energy and holding onto it intentionally within your home. First, we looked at Feng Shui's history and power, set intentions for your home and became friendly with it. You reflected on how you were treating your home and began to connect with its soul. Once discovered, you set to work releasing old negative physical and emotional clutter that was holding you back, and clearing space for new intentions to flow in. Next, you mapped your home according to classical Feng Shui, moving area by area through your home to relate each space to each of the nine life areas or Power Centres, learning the enhancements for each. After intentionally enhancing these Feng Shui areas, you move on to looking at your home through the lens of each room's energy, maximising the opportunity for good energy to flow and minimising the risk of stagnant or negative energies dragging you down. Finally, you took a peek into some particularly auspicious aspects of Feng Shui, looking at art and money.

Along the way, I hope you've been journaling your heart out, noticing, noticing, noticing the correlation between your living areas and the decluttering and enhancing you have invested in. It may have been subtle or it may have been sublime. Whatever changes you have seen in

Patricia Lohan

your life, know that there is so much more where that came from.

To embrace Feng Shui to the max and harness the **personal energy** of your home, you can now start to take it further. Why personalise? Feng Shui is not a generic art. Every home has its own specific energetic blueprint. Just like no two humans have the same fingerprint, no two homes' energies are alike. In the same way, you have a unique energy signature based on your birth date and time, your home is also one-of-a-kind. It has its own personality, history, and imprint on the world. You may be able to apply changes that are generally good for your home, yet the complexity of layers of Feng Shui means that there comes a time when the exact combination for your home needs some fine-tuning. To harness the **full potential** of the energy of your home (and the impact it has on your life), you benefit most from a deep level of Feng Shui practice.

This deeper level is far beyond what I can teach in a book. In fact, it is far beyond the scope of any book. To experience this, you need personalised attention, starting with assessing how you are doing so.

In other words, with all the changes you've been making, what has worked and where are you still stuck?

One element of Feng Shui which blows my mind is that your house is one of four types; Good for People & Good for Money, Good for People & Bad For Money, Bad for People & Good for Money or Bad for Money & People.

Whichever house yours is, it's directly impacting what is going on in your life — either attracting what you want or repelling it. The question is which house type is yours?

Is your home good for people but bad for money? Have you welcomed financial abundance but seen your relationships take a nose-dive or simply stagnate? Is your house a money magnet or money repellent? Is your house a supportive home or an unsupportive home? Find out your house type by answering yes or no to these quick quiz questions below.

EXERCISE: HOUSE TYPE QUIZ

Let's explore the next steps through the lens of what's working in your home by answering a few simple questions. You can do the quiz here, or online at www. patricialohan.com/quiz

Money

1. *Does money flow easily into your home?*
2. *Do you have a healthy savings account?*
3. *Can you always afford the things you want?*
4. *Since you moved into this house, have your finances improved?*
5. *Does your home feel luxurious and first class?*
6. *Have you had any unexpected financial windfalls?*
7. *Can you pay all your household bills with ease?*

If you responded **mostly yeses**, your house is good for money.

If you answered **mostly noes**, it's bad for money.

People

1. *Do your spirits fall when you walk into your home?*
2. *Is there constant bickering and arguments in your home?*
3. *Do things break regularly?*
4. *Do you feel unsupported by your home?*
5. *Do you sometimes feel like you are jinxed, and that unexpected negative things happen out of the blue?*
6. *Have you experienced any, or all, of the following: legal suits, addictive behaviour, robbery, leaks?*
7. *Are unexpected accidents and illnesses a regular occurrence in your home?*

If you answered **mostly yeses**, your home is bad for people.

If you had *mostly noes*, it's good for people.

House types

There are four different house types:

Good for People — Good for Money

Lucky you! Life seems to be going great. Your abundance and happy relationships appear to be going well and improving. You have an opportunity to start personalising straight away and allow that good fortune to flow even more freely. There is always room for some improvement, right? Keep going. You're doing great.

Good for People — Bad for Money

Wow! What a happy home you have. But money can be a bit 'tricky' over at your place. If this seems like a bit of a shock, don't panic. You can turn around your money luck and I can show you how. Worrying about money isn't any fun. If you just had your money worries sorted, wouldn't life be amazing?

Bad for People — Good for Money

As the old saying goes 'money doesn't buy happiness'. It's great to have all this abundance, but it's not all rosy in the house when you are at home. Don't worry. This crazy stuff going on isn't your fault and it can be turned around. Let's see if you can create a little more peace at your place.

Bad for People — Bad for Money

Having this house type is such a huge opportunity for you because you now have the awareness that any crap stuff going on in your life is not your fault. The house you are living in could be causing many of the negative experiences to happen. And now you know about it, you can do something about it. The good news is, you can transform this space into somewhere much happier and luckier.

Whatever your home type, know that right now you have the opportunity to turn around your fortune and improve the flow of prosperity and happy people in your life. With the power of Feng Shui, any and every house can become good for both money and people. The questions you have just answered can be used as an indicator of the type of house you live in, but a deeper analysis of your exact house type will be required when you go to the next level of personalisation, where I highly recommend the involvement of a trained professional.

Fiona's Story

Fiona is a powerful lightworker, and was living in a good for people and bad for money house. She found as soon as she and her husband started making changes to the house, their business luck turned around rapidly.

> *"For me, it's been a game-changer. The income has increased, but so has what I'm doing to generate that income. That is the blessing. I'm no*

longer slogging away at work that was so unrewarding. I am mostly doing healing and transformational work with my clients, and clients that are showing up for me to work with. I love and adore them! There is just more money and more happiness. And that's the biggest thing."

Before doing the programme, Fiona had all the tools, but something wasn't clicking.

"If there's something you're struggling with in your life and you want to make a change, you've got to change the environment you're in so that it's all aligned with what you want, and so there's flow.

You might have all the tools, or maybe you need to get more education, or something has to shift in that way, but if you don't shift your environment to align with it, you'll only ever get so far, and there might be a lot more effort and struggle than there needs to actually be."

CHAPTER 34

The Big Obstacle

The biggest obstacle we notice with our members who start their journey with Feng Shui is whether or not they are willing to put in the effort. This resistance mainly has to do with deep-seated beliefs of worthiness around living their best life. It can be difficult to take action if an unconscious belief is holding you back.

People will often read this book and imagine the idea of living in a Feng Shui-ed home, and living their dream life. But many people will encounter resistance in themselves when it comes to taking that first step toward their dreams.

When you read this book, you might find yourself stumbling when creating a floor plan for your home, taking a compass reading, or filling out your home questionnaire. It could be the case that your sceptical husband might be against you, or your friends might see Feng Shui as a waste of time and energy.

The biggest roadblock we have noticed is in the implementation of the Feng Shui and members who might feel a lack of support in their lives.

But this is where the PowerHouse programme steps in. The biggest advantage you'll have as one of our members is being a part of our community. We have an easily accessible online group of women who are just like you, who log on every day to share their Feng Shui experience.

Our group is full of daily wins, shares and support, which make everyone feel that they are not on their own and that they are a part of something bigger.

Every day, questions get answered in our Facebook group by myself and our PowerHouse Feng Shui-trained consultants. So you'll always have support, no matter what.

And we've seen it time and time again — members will join with tons of sceptical people in their lives, but somewhere along the way, we'll see a post in our group that goes something like this, *"You won't believe it! Yesterday, my sceptical husband asked me for Feng Shui advice for a job interview he's going to next week."*

Jennifer's Story

Jennifer is a PowerHouse member who lives in Queens, New York. She joined our programme with the intention of finding love in her life.

She took about two months to implement all of her Feng Shui remedies and do all the work in the programme. Even though she joined PowerHouse with the intention of finding a partner, she found that she just totally fell in love with her home!

> *"I just freaking love my apartment! It's so amazing. After implementing my Feng Shui, there is just so much more alignment in all areas of my life. When I got my report, it said that my home was Good for Money and Bad for People. I thought that made a lot of sense. And while money wasn't a problem, there's just so much more money flowing into my world right now!*
>
> *Besides just being in love with my apartment, I have met someone and it's gotten pretty serious. It's only been six months, and it feels like an amazing relationship."*

This is so cool! So Jennifer basically has aligned herself with her original intention of bringing love into her home, but everything else in her life has also come into better balance.

> **"Making money is something I've always been good at, but it's always come from a place of manic. It was not necessarily healthy. My relationship with work and making money is way easier now.**
>
> **It's just getting your home to work with you instead of against you. It's not rocket science. I feel that Feng Shui is something that will be a part of my life forever. The support you get from it is just so awesome and amazing. Life just feels better."**

CHAPTER 35

Your Next Steps

Yay, you have gotten this far! And I hope that you've taken lots of notes and started taking action and implementing my suggestions to create a Happy Home for you and your family.

Feng Shui is a continuous journey of growth and self-discovery.

It might seem a bit overwhelming knowing where to start, but that's where this checklist comes in, and working through it will help you check through each room in your home making sure it is Happy Feng Shui!

You can download it here: www.patricialohan.com/happyhomebonuses

And, as I reassure my clients and participants of PowerHouse — you don't need to do it all today. You are in your home for the long haul, this is a marathon and not a sprint. Take it one step at a time; your house, your family, and your life will feel the benefits.

I'd love to see you over in my community of incredible women all working on raising the vibration of their homes to attract infinite abundance and joy.

My Wish For You

My wish for you is that you live in the happiest of homes. That it is a harmonious home. For you to be living your dreams awake. For your entire home to be supporting you in every aspect of your life. So that you can flourish, grow, and be the divine, beautiful being that you are meant to be. That your family are getting along great, that everything is easy and joyful.

I want you to live in a home where your spirit rises when you walk in. A home you feel totally supported by, that you feel aligned to its environment, and that there's a daily sense of tapping into flow. That life just flows easily for you through your home.

That you are in a home that supports you.

What To Do Next

Ready for the next level?

We have many free resources that you can explore www. patricialohan.com/happyhomebonuses for example

- Soul of Your Home meditation
- Action Steps checklist
- Consider becoming a PowerHouse member

Now that you've reflected on how far you've come and have an indication of your house type, you will have an idea of the potential of your home to change the happiness, health, wealth, relationships, success, fame, and fortune in your life. So, if you're at the end of this book and you've seen some amazing results and heard some incredible real-life stories, how can you know for sure that you're ready for more personalisation or whether you should just stick where you are?

When you're ready to activate greater health, wealth, and happiness in every area of life and you've expended your current resources for achieving those dreams, you may feel like:

- You are unsupported in one or several areas of your life
- You've tried everything
- You're in a cycle of one step forward, two steps back

- You were just lucky when a few things started to change
- You've been stuck in an area for so long that you don't believe anything could work
- Your life isn't that bad and you should stick with what you've got
- You've done loads of self-improvement and it hasn't worked

No matter how hard you try, some areas just won't click or will take more work and perseverance. Until you deal with your environment energetically and personally, you'll never have the kind of abundance or success that you truly dream about; the kind of abundance and success that you hardly dare admit to yourself. This is why, when you're ready to dive deep, deep, deep into creating a life that is aligned and feels incredible from the inside out, you have to apply Feng Shui at a deeper, more specific personal level.

What personalised Feng Shui looks like

As you have heard stories throughout the book I offer my signature programme called PowerHouse that looks at specific prescriptive measures to ensure your home's unique needs and remedies are addressed. We analyse the hidden invisible energies flowing in your home. I've seen first-hand the extraordinary power of personalising. To be honest, the reason I created the course was because friends and family kept asking me how I was able to attract the wealth, abundance, support, relationship, and fame that I'd been wanting into my life and how I'd done it so quickly, easily, and joyfully. Let's face it, they knew me as that single, broke, bike-borrowing, couch-surfing, yoga-teaching woman I was not so long ago.

So now that I've worked with so many women who have also had enormous leaps forward and become super specific with their Feng Shui journey, let me explain what personalised, specific, prescriptive Feng Shui looks like.

This personalised kind of Feng Shui is so unique. It relies on professionally assessing every aspect of your home using photos, the year of construction, and more compass readings. It means identifying the specific invisible energies flowing through your home and learning exactly how you can work with them with detailed cures and enhancers, which can be as simple as a purple comforter on your bed like Talmar.

Personalised Feng Shui works with the elements, and with symbols, colours, crystals, and gemstones to bring balance to the energy of your home. You can expect rapid — often dramatic — shifts in the energy of your life.

Next steps

If you've taken action on what you've learned in this book, and had a look at your results of the quiz if you haven't done it already do it here www.patricialohan.com/quiz, I'd love to have you part of our amazing community and living in a home that supports you 100%. I've poured all my years of accumulated knowledge and experience into it. It's highly personalised and interactive, with a fabulous community, so you can make rapid improvements in any area of your life. Specifically, as a part of the course, you will get what you need in which you, your family, and even a business can flourish! After working with people from around the world and seeing their results, I can assure you that Feng Shui is the stuff of dreams coming true; unlocking the flow of good stuff to you in your life.

So whatever your dream — that's my dream for you too! I believe we all deserve and are worthy of creating lives that are abundant, easy and flowing. Feng Shui in my experience enables all this and more is possible when you have a home that supports you! You have read, throughout this book, the success stories of my wonderful women who introduced Feng Shui into their homes and lives. I'd love to be sharing your success stories in my next book!

We'd love your feedback from your time exploring this book. Follow us on Instagram to share your stories and connect with us!

You can check it out
www.patricialohan.com/powerhouse
www.instagram.com/powerhousefengshui

Thank you so much for coming this far in creating your own happy, healthy, wealthy home. I wish you love and luck for your onward journey.

Patricia xxx

ABOUT THE AUTHOR

Patricia Lohan is the international best-selling author of *The Happy Home: Your Guide To Creating A Happy, Healthy, Wealthy Life and How to Become a PowerHouse in Business using Feng Shui.* Patricia Lohan helps women make their homes magnetic to money, luck, and blessings. She shows you what they don't teach in schools, what lies between the lines, and what her top-secret tools are for success. She is a Feng Shui expert, a healer, and a passionate female entrepreneur who has shaped her dream life, living between Bali, Greece, New York, Italy and Ireland with her husband. Patricia has a gift for making Feng Shui simple and easy to understand and implement.

She has helped thousands of people across the globe embrace Feng Shui and creates lasting changes in their homes, lives, and businesses. Patricia has seen first-hand the power of the mind, surroundings, and inner-healing, clearing and aligning everything so it works holistically.

Check out her top Feng Shui Tips at www.patricia lohan.com

Follow her on Instagram www.instagram.com/ patricialohan

ACKNOWLEDGEMENTS

As I taught and shared my passion for Feng Shui, more and more people said I should write a book.

Thank you to all of you for requesting this book.

You know who you are.

I am SO excited for people to embrace Feng Shui, something that has totally transformed my life for the better, and that of the thousands of women I have supported in my PowerHouse course and through my free training programmes.

Thank you for your patience with me on this journey.

Thank you to my family and friends for your continued support and encouragement.

Thank you to all my clients and the participants of PowerHouse — it's your incredible success stories, transformations, and dedication to creating a better life that spurs me on every day.

To all my teachers and mentors.

To my incredible team who have facilitated all my crazy ideas and help me get Feng Shui out into the world every day.

I am SO grateful for my biggest personal Feng Shui success; meeting my amazing husband, Ken who has tirelessly supported me on this journey.

I LOVE our adventures together and how, one house at a time, we are changing the world for the better.

And of course Toby, thank you for your big kisses, cuddles unconditional love.